QUICK & EASY

QUICK & EASY

Over **140** delicious recipes, **500** color photographs, **STEP-BY-STEP** images, and **NUTRITIONAL INFORMATION**

This edition published in 2012
LOVE FOOD is an imprint of Parragon Books Ltd

Parragon
Queen Street House
4 Queen Street
Bath BA1 1HE, UK

www.parragon.com

ISBN: 978-1-4454-6573-9

Printed in China

Cover and additional design by Geoff Borin
New photography by Clive Bozzard-Hill
New home economy by Valerie Barrett
New recipes and introduction by Christine France
Notes by Sarah Bush
Edited by Fiona Biggs
Nutritional analysis by Fiona Hunter

Notes for the Reader
This book uses standard kitchen measuring spoons and cups. All spoon and cup
measurements are level unless otherwise indicated. Unless otherwise stated,
milk is assumed to be whole, eggs are large, individual vegetables are medium,
and pepper is freshly ground black pepper. Unless otherwise stated, all root
vegetables should be washed and peeled before using.

Garnishes, decorations and serving suggestions are all optional and not
necessarily included in the recipe ingredients or method. Any optional
ingredients and seasoning to taste are not included in the nutritional analysis.
The times given are only an approximate guide. Preparation times differ
according to the techniques used by different people and the cooking times
may also vary from those given. Optional ingredients, variations, or serving
suggestions have not been included in the calculations.

Recipes using raw or very lightly cooked eggs should be avoided by infants, the
elderly, pregnant women, and people with weakened immune systems. Pregnant
and breast-feeding women are advised to avoid eating peanuts and peanut
products. People with nut allergies should be aware that some of the prepared
ingredients used in the recipes in this book may contain nuts. Always check the
packaging before use.

Vegetarians should be aware that some of the prepared ingredients used in the
recipes in this book may contain animal products. Always check the package
before use.

Contents

Cooking fast and fresh

There's no doubt that cooking can be a rewarding activity, especially when there is time to enjoy the process. These days, however, many people are often so busy that few folk have the option to spend hours in the kitchen, and sometimes cooking everyday meals can eat away too much valuable time. In addition, if you're tired at the end of a long day's work, cooking can become just another chore, especially if all you really want is a quick, easy meal solution. Instead of reaching for the TV dinners and feeling guilty, what you need are methods for making the best of fresh, healthy foods, simply prepared and cooked in as short a time as possible. That's why you will find this book invaluable.

You'll find the following pages filled with an impressive variety of appetizing ideas for easy dishes for every meal of the day, from breakfast to dinner, all of which need the absolute minimum of preparation. These recipes will not just save you time and effort, but they'll save you money, too—it's much less expensive to make your own meals from fresh ingredients than to buy prepared TV dinners. You'll also have the peace of mind that comes from knowing that you've cooked a healthy, nutritious meal from fresh, seasonal foods without hidden additives or unhealthy ingredients. You'll know exactly what's in the dishes you're serving to your friends and family.

Not only are all the recipes really quick and simple to prepare and cook, but the recipes come with the added bonus of plenty of useful hints and tips, offering advice on how to vary a recipe for a change of pace, or to make the most of seasonal alternatives. There are also tips for success, handy time-saving hints, nutritional information and healthy tips, useful serving suggestions, and advice on how to freeze each dish.

Colorful fresh vegetables make quick and easy midweek meals that can often be cooked in one pan, saving dishwashing time, too!

Make each meal special. Turn simple recipes into a feast for the eyes by choosing attractive dishes, place settings, and napkins.

Laid out in a clear, simple, step-by-step format, all the recipes are designed to be easy-to-follow at a glance, with helpful photographs to guide you through each step of the way and a beautiful color image of every finished dish. Plus, we've made sure each complete recipe fits on one spread so you'll never need to turn the page in the middle of a recipe.

We've included some familiar old favorites such as Speedy Spaghetti Bolognese and Chocolate Pudding, plus lots of new recipe ideas to keep your menus fresh and varied. Soon, you'll find you can use the recipes as a reliable basis to start experimenting with your own variations and ideas, adding your own special touches to make them truly individual and seasonal.

The secrets of successful quick-and-easy cooking

Get the basics right

● Keep kitchen countertops tidy, so when you're ready to cook, you have the space to work properly. Even the smallest kitchen can be an excellent work space if it's organized properly.

● Keep useful pieces of equipment, such as food processors or immersion blenders in an easily accessed place. They won't save you time if they are hidden in a cupboard. Processors can be bulky but they're great time-savers, so make counter space for yours and you'll use it more often.

● Sharpen your knives—a sharp knife cuts far more efficiently, and safely, than a blunt one. Store them safely in a knife block or rack.

● If possible, attach a rack on the wall for handy preparation tools, such as whisks, peelers, or slotted spoons, so they're always within reach instead of you having to rifle through the kitchen drawers.

Getting organized

● Before you start to cook, always read through the recipe.

● Be realistic about timing—check the preparation and cooking times, decide when you want to serve the meal, then work backwards to calculate what time you need to start.

● Assemble all the ingredients and measure out as needed, and be sure any special equipment is ready to use.

● Preheat the oven or broiler before starting. Most ovens can take 10–15 minutes to heat up to the required temperature. Some recipes also suggest preheating a baking sheet in the oven, which will speed up cooking times.

● Clean up as you go, putting away items and quickly wiping clean any surfaces, ready for the next step.

● Have a dishpan of hot, soapy water ready to put items into so they will be easy to rinse later on. You can always load the dishwasher while the dish cooks.

Choose the right tools and equipment, and preparing meals will be enjoyable instead of being a chore.

Time-saving tips

- Use kitchen scissors to snip foods such as scallions, chives, and bacon–this is quicker than chopping them with a knife.

- When vegetables such as carrots or potatoes are young and fresh, there's no need to peel them because the skins are tender—in fact, they're more nutritious this way. Just rinse or scrub off any dirt and trim off damaged parts.

- If you're just crushing one clove of garlic with a garlic crusher, there's no need to skin the garlic before crushing—the crusher will be easier to clean, too.

- Have a few standby staples on hand, such as jars of prepared sauces and straight-to-wok noodles, for when time is really tight, so you'll just need to add some fresh ingredients for an easy meal.

- If you have extra time when shredding cheese, chopping herbs, or making bread crumbs, prepare extra to store in the freezer; this will save time on another day.

- Add small amounts of leftover wine to ice-cube trays and freeze, ready to add to dishes later.

- Use a microwave to speed up defrosting foods, or for melting chocolate, softening butter for creaming, etc.

Fast foods for easy meals

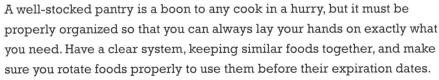

A well-stocked pantry is a boon to any cook in a hurry, but it must be properly organized so that you can always lay your hands on exactly what you need. Have a clear system, keeping similar foods together, and make sure you rotate foods properly to use them before their expiration dates.

Your refrigerator also needs to be organized, so that you can see what you have and find foods easily. Generally speaking, you should keep raw foods at the bottom and cooked at the top. So, dairy produce is best stored on the top shelf, and uncooked meat, chicken, and fish should be covered on the bottom shelf.

Pasta and pizza—so quick to prepare and great standby meals when everyone's really hungry.

Pantry basics

- Flavorings such as vanilla or lemon extract, are easier to use than steeping vanilla beans or grating zest when time is tight.

- Pasta and rice are great for quick meals, but consider also keeping other grains, such as couscous, for variety.

- Bouillon cubes or powder are useful for adding flavor when you don't have time to prepare freshly made stock.

- Canned beans, such as red kidney beans, chickpeas, and pinto beans, save hours of soaking and simmering dried beans. Add straight to casseroles and stews, or toss in a well-flavored dressing for a quick salad.

- Canned tomatoes, tomato paste, and tomato puree or tomato sauce are a must for any pantry, to go in all kinds of casseroles, stews, soups, and pizzas.

Getting your kitchen organized so you know what you have in the pantry and refrigerator and where equipment is will be a huge help when it comes to putting a meal on the table quickly.

Time-saving standbys

• Jars of green and red pesto are great for adding instant rich Mediterranean flavors to casseroles, pasta, baked or broiled meat and fish, pizzas, sauces, and soups. Once opened, store in the refrigerator or freezer.

• Good-quality flavored oils, such as chili oil, hazelnut oil, or walnut oil, are a wonderful quick way to add a last-minute flourish to plain, bland dishes.

• Prepared pizza crusts or pita bread, stored in the freezer, can be topped with your choice of fresh toppings and baked in minutes.

• Straight-to-wok noodles are great for quick stir-fries and Asian dishes, and remember also that dried egg noodles and rice noodles take only a few minutes to cook—and they're cheaper, too.

• A fresh avocado is always worth having on hand—put one in the fruit bowl to ripen quickly, so it will be ready to use in dips, sandwiches, salads, or as a quick appetizer.

• Fresh lemons are invaluable for all kinds of dishes and garnishes. Store them in a plastic food bag in the crisper drawer of your refrigerator, and they'll keep well for at least a week.

Speedy preparation tips

• To peel garlic quickly and easily, place a clove on a board and press firmly with the flat side of a large chef's knife—the peel should slip off easily.

• Make speedy salad dressings in a screw-topped jar—simply put all the ingredients in the jar, screw the lid on firmly, and shake well.

• To coat pieces of meat or fish in flour or spices, put the coating ingredients in a plastic food bag, add the pieces of food, and shake well to coat evenly.

Time-saving equipment

There's absolutely no need for a huge collection of expensive gadgets for quick-and-easy cooking, but a few basic items can be extremely useful. Start with these:

A handheld electric mixer doesn't take up much room and you will find it a great time-saver when making cakes.

Food processor

A processor with a powerful motor is a good investment for any kitchen, and can be a great time-saver, invaluable for speedy pureeing, blending, chopping, slicing, and grating. Most models have a special blade for creaming mixtures and for kneading bread doughs.

Microwave

Use a microwave oven to cut timings on all kinds of food preparation. Use on a low or defrost setting to soften butter to use for baking or spreading, or to defrost frozen foods. Microwaves are also great for making quick sauces such as hollandaise, cooking scrambled eggs and oatmeal, melting ingredients such as chocolate, or for steaming vegetables or fish.

Handheld immersion blender

A small handheld immersion blender is handy for pureeing small amounts of mixture and for blending soups or sauces in the saucepan. To clean easily, unplug and shake the blades in a bowl of soapy water, then rinse under the faucet and let air-dry.

Handheld electric mixer

This gadget is ideal for whisking egg whites or cream, beating cake batters, or smoothing out sauces. These often also have a dough hook that can be used for kneading small amounts of bread dough. Choose one with a powerful motor for the best results.

Electrical kitchen aids will complete some of the more tedious preparation stages of recipes quickly, so take time to choose the right one for your needs.

Time-saving extras

• A good-quality swivel-blade vegetable peeler is a valuable small tool for speedy peeling of vegetables—it's not only quicker than a knife, but peels more thinly, retaining maximum nutrients.

• A stiff vegetable brush can eliminate the need for peeling altogether—try this with young root vegetables such as potatoes or carrots.

• A garlic crusher can also be used for crushing fresh ginger.

• Reusable nonstick liners for baking sheets and baking pans make baking easier and there's no need to grease.

• Precut parchment liners will save time lining cake pans—buy a selection of the sizes you use most frequently.

Quick tips

• Use a large kitchen spoon to scoop out the flesh from a ripe avocado, without peeling.

• If it doesn't seem worth using a processor to process a small amount of, for example, herbs or bread crumbs, prepare a larger quantity than you need and freeze the rest to save time another day.

• Use an ice-cream scoop to quickly measure meatballs and cookie dough so that they're all the same size.

• To keep the inside of your microwave clean, cover foods that may spatter by placing a sheet of paper towel loosely over the top.

• To clean the inside of a microwave easily, stir 2 tablespoons of baking soda in 1 cup of water in a microwave-safe container, then cook on high for 3 minutes. Wipe the surfaces with paper towels.

Greek Yogurt with Honey, Nuts & Blueberries 18

Muesli 20

French Toast 22

Eggs Benedict with Quick Hollandaise Sauce 24

Blueberry Pancakes with Whipped Butter 26

Silver Dollar Pancakes with Maple Syrup 28

Quick Tomato Soup 30

Quick Chunky Vegetable Soup 32

Leek & Potato Soup 34

Spicy Beef & Noodle Soup 36

Chicken & Summer Vegetable Soup 38

Chili Beef Stir-Fry 40

Bacon, Lettuce & Tomato Salad 42

Honey & Chicken Pasta Salad 44

Lentil & Tuna Salad 46

Tomato, Olive & Mozzarella Pasta Salad 48

Avocado Salad with Lime Dressing 50

Cheese Steak Baguette 52

Meatball Sub 54

Paprika Steak Wraps with Horseradish Cream 56

Smoked Chicken & Ham Focaccia 58

Turkey Wraps with Brie & Cranberry 60

Hot Salmon, Tomato & Cream Cheese on a Bagel 62

Mini Muffin Pizzas 64

Roasted Vegetable & Feta Cheese Wraps 66

Brunch & Light Bites

Greek Yogurt with Honey, Nuts & Blueberries

 SERVES 4 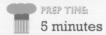 PREP TIME: 5 minutes   COOKING TIME: 5 minutes

nutritional information per serving	263 cal, 17g fat, 4g sat fat, 18g total sugars, 0.15g salt

Greek yogurt, with its rich, velvety texture and creamy taste, is the perfect choice for this wonderful breakfast treat. If you're watching your weight, look for a low-fat version, which will still taste great!

INGREDIENTS

3 tablespoons honey
¾ cup mixed unsalted nuts
½ cup Greek yogurt
1⅓ cups fresh blueberries

1. Heat the honey in a small saucepan over medium heat, add the nuts, and stir until they are well coated. Remove from the heat and let cool slightly.

2. Divide the yogurt among four serving bowls, then spoon the nut mixture and blueberries over the yogurt. Serve immediately.

SOMETHING DIFFERENT
For a change, top the yogurt with raspberries, strawberries, or sliced bananas.

Muesli

 SERVES 4　　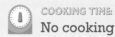 PREP TIME: 10 minutes　　 COOKING TIME: No cooking

nutritional information
per serving | 316 cal, 14g fat, 2g sat fat, 14g total sugars, trace salt

*This chunky muesli mixture is not just for breakfast—
it's a nutritious snack, too.*

INGREDIENTS

1 ¼ cups rolled oats
½ cup diced dried apricots
¼ cup coarsely chopped pecans
⅓ cup golden raisins
¼ cup dried cranberries
4 teaspoons pumpkin seeds
5 teaspoons sunflower seeds
1 tablespoon sesame seeds
yogurt or milk, to serve

1. Put the oats in a large mixing bowl. Stir in the apricots, nuts, golden raisins, cranberries, and seeds, mixing well to combine evenly.

2. Store the muesli in an airtight container until needed. Serve with yogurt.

HEALTHY HINT
Stir in a freshly grated apple or pear before serving to add natural sweetness, extra fiber, and vitamins. Keep the skin on for maximum nutrients.

French Toast

 SERVES 6

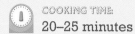 PREP TIME: 10 minutes

COOKING TIME: 20–25 minutes

nutritional information per serving	374 cal, 21g fat, 9g sat fat, 3g total sugars, 1.3g salt

How could something as simple as bread soaked in eggs and fried taste so delicious? Maybe the warm, fragrant maple syrup is the answer!

INGREDIENTS

6 eggs

¾ cup milk

¼ teaspoon ground cinnamon

12 slices day-old plain white bread

about 4 tablespoons butter or margarine, plus extra to serve

½–1 tablespoon sunflower oil or vegetable oil

salt

warm maple syrup, to serve

1. Break the eggs into a large, shallow bowl, beat together with the milk and cinnamon, and season with salt

2. Add the bread slices and press them down so that they are covered on both sides with the egg mixture. Let the bread stand for 1–2 minutes to soak up the egg mixture, turning the slices over once.

3. Melt half the butter with half the oil in a large skillet. Add as many bread slices to the skillet as will fit in a single layer and cook for 2–3 minutes, until golden brown.

4. Turn the bread slices over and cook on the other side until golden brown. Repeat this process with the remaining bread, adding extra butter and oil to the skillet if necessary, while keeping the cooked French toast warm. Serve the French toast in stacks with butter and maple syrup.

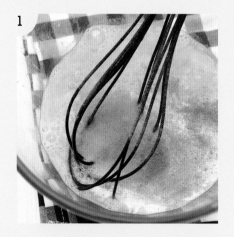

1

2

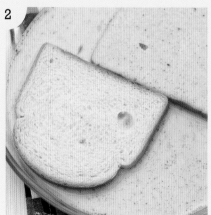

3

Eggs Benedict with Quick Hollandaise Sauce

 SERVES 4    PREP TIME: 5 minutes   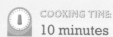 COOKING TIME: 10 minutes

nutritional information per serving	699 cal, 54g fat, 30g sat fat, 3g total sugars, 2.3g salt

The perfect dish for a lazy Sunday brunch. This will keep everyone happy.

INGREDIENTS

1 tablespoon white-wine vinegar
4 eggs
4 English muffins
4 slices good-quality ham

quick hollandaise sauce
3 egg yolks
1¾ sticks butter
1 tablespoon lemon juice
pepper

1. To poach the eggs, fill a saucepan three-quarters full with water and bring to a boil over low heat. Reduce the heat to a simmer and add the vinegar. When the water is barely simmering, carefully break the eggs into the skillet. Poach the eggs for 3 minutes, or until the whites are just set but the yolks are still soft.

2. Meanwhile, to make the hollandaise sauce, put the egg yolks in a food processor or blender. Melt the butter in a small saucepan until bubbling. With the motor running, gradually add the hot butter to the food processor in a steady stream until the sauce is thick and creamy. Add the lemon juice, and a little warm water if the sauce is too thick, then season with pepper. Remove from the food processor and keep warm.

3. Split the muffins and toast them on both sides. Top each muffin with a slice of ham, a poached egg, and a generous spoonful of hollandaise sauce. Season with more pepper, if desired, and serve immediately.

Blueberry Pancakes with Whipped Butter

 SERVES 4  PREP TIME: 15 minutes  COOKING TIME: 15 minutes

nutritional information per serving 528 cal, 35g fat, 18g sat fat, 17g total sugars, 0.8g salt

A stack of freshly made pancakes, blueberries, butter, and syrup will get your day off to a good start!

INGREDIENTS

1¼ cups all-purpose flour

1½ teaspoons baking powder

pinch of salt

2 tablespoons sugar

1 cup milk

1 extra-large egg

2 tablespoons sunflower oil, plus extra for greasing

1 cup blueberries, plus extra to decorate

whipped butter

1 stick unsalted butter, at room temperature

2 tablespoons milk

1 tablespoon maple syrup, plus extra to serve

1. For the whipped butter, put the butter in a bowl and beat with an electric mixer until softened. Add the milk and maple syrup and beat hard until pale and fluffy.

2. Sift the flour, baking powder, salt, and sugar into a bowl. Add the milk, egg, and oil and beat to a smooth batter. Stir in the blueberries and let stand for 5 minutes.

3. Lightly grease a griddle pan or skillet and heat over medium heat. Spoon tablespoons of batter into the pan and cook until bubbles appear on the surface. Turn over with a spatula and cook the other side until golden brown. Repeat this process using the remaining batter, while keeping the cooked pancakes warm.

4. Serve the pancakes in stacks with extra blueberries, a spoonful of whipped butter, and a drizzle of maple syrup.

FREEZING TIP

Make pancakes omitting the fruit. Cool, wrap in plastic wrap, and freeze in an airtight bag for up to 1 month. Thaw, then heat on a baking sheet in a warm oven. Serve with fresh fruit.

Silver Dollar Pancakes with Maple Syrup

 SERVES 6  PREP TIME: 10 minutes  COOKING TIME: 10 minutes

nutritional information per serving	200 cal, 6g fat, 3g sat fat, 11g total sugars, 0.6g salt

The buttermilk in the batter gives the pancakes a light and airy texture.

INGREDIENTS

1¼ cups all-purpose flour
1½ teaspoons baking powder
pinch of salt
1 cup buttermilk
1 extra-large egg
2 tablespoons melted butter
sunflower oil, for greasing
maple syrup, to serve

1. Sift the flour, baking powder, and salt into a bowl. Add the buttermilk, egg, and butter and beat to a smooth batter. Let stand for 5 minutes.

2. Lightly grease a griddle pan or skillet and heat over medium heat. Spoon small spoonfuls of batter into the pan to make pancakes approximately 1½ inches wide and cook until bubbles appear on the surface.

3. Turn over with a spatula and cook the other side until golden brown. Repeat this process using the remaining batter, while keeping the cooked pancakes warm.

4. Serve the pancakes in tall stacks, drizzled with maple syrup.

SOMETHING DIFFERENT

Serve the pancakes topped with smoked salmon, a grind of black pepper, a squeeze of lemon juice, and a blob of sour cream for a special treat!

Quick Tomato Soup

 SERVES 4   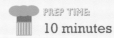 PREP TIME: 10 minutes   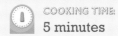 COOKING TIME: 5 minutes

nutritional information per serving	100 cal, 6g fat, 0.8g sat fat, 5g total sugars, 0.4g salt

This is a great staple standby that's ready in minutes and makes a delicious lunch. At an adult dinner party, try adding a splash of vodka to the soup before sering.

INGREDIENTS

2 tablespoons olive oil

1 large onion, chopped

1¾ cups of canned peeled plum tomatoes

1¼ cups chicken stock or vegetable stock

1 tablespoon tomato paste

1 teaspoon hot chili sauce

handful of fresh basil leaves

salt and pepper

slices of bread, to serve

1. Heat the oil in a large saucepan over medium heat, add the onion, and sauté for 4–5 minutes, stirring, until soft.

2. Add the tomatoes with their can juices, stock, tomato paste, chili sauce, and half the basil leaves. Puree with an immersion blender, or process in a food processor or blender, until smooth, and return to the pan.

3. Stir the soup over medium heat until just boiling, then season with salt and pepper.

4. Transfer the soup to warm serving bowls. Garnish with the remaining basil leaves and serve immediately with slices of bread.

Quick Chunky Vegetable Soup

 SERVES 4   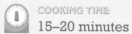 PREP TIME: 10 minutes   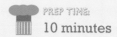 COOKING TIME: 15–20 minutes

nutritional information per serving	113 cal, 6g fat, 0.7g sat fat, 8g total sugars, 0.3g salt

This is a hearty, satisfying soup that makes a colorful and nutritious lunch any day of the week.

INGREDIENTS

1 red onion
1 celery stalk
1 zucchini
2 carrots
2 tablespoons sunflower oil
1 (14½-ounce) can diced tomatoes
1¼ cups chicken stock or vegetable stock
large sprig of fresh thyme
salt and pepper
chopped thyme, to garnish
rolls, to serve

1. Cut the onion, celery, zucchini, and carrots into ½-inch cubes.

2. Heat the oil in a large saucepan over medium heat. Add the vegetables and sauté, stirring, for 5 minutes without browning.

3. Add the tomatoes, stock, and the thyme sprig. Bring to a boil, then reduce the heat. Cover and simmer for 10–15 minutes, until the vegetables are just tender. Remove the thyme sprig and season with salt and pepper.

4. Transfer the soup to warm serving bowls. Garnish with chopped thyme and serve immediately with rolls.

Leek & Potato Soup

 SERVES 4    PREP TIME: 10 minutes    COOKING TIME: 20 minutes

nutritional information per serving | 253 cal, 19g fat, 12g sat fat, 4g total sugars, 0.2g salt

This is one of the world's greatest recipes, combining two favorite vegetables in a smooth, creamy soup. As well as being a great choice for cold weather, it tastes wonderful served chilled in the summer, too.

INGREDIENTS

4 tablespoons butter
1 onion, chopped
3 leeks, sliced
2 potatoes, cut into ¾-inch cubes
3½ cups vegetable stock
salt and pepper
⅔ cup light cream and
2 tablespoons snipped fresh chives, to garnish
rolls, to serve

1. Melt the butter in a large saucepan over medium heat, add the onion, leeks, and potatoes and sauté gently for 2–3 minutes, until soft but not brown.

2. Pour in the stock, bring to a boil, then reduce the heat and simmer, covered, for 15 minutes.

3. Puree with an immersion blender or transfer to a food processor or blender, process until smooth, and return to the pan. Heat the soup gently and season with salt and pepper.

4. Transfer the soup to warm serving bowls. Garnish with cream and chives and serve immediately with rolls.

Spicy Beef & Noodle Soup

 SERVES 4   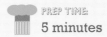 PREP TIME: 5 minutes    COOKING TIME: 10 minutes

nutritional information per serving	324 cal, 16g fat, 3g sat fat, 7g total sugars, 4.8g salt

Bring the taste of Thailand to your kitchen with this fragrant soup, which is also quick to make.

INGREDIENTS

4¼ pints beef stock

⅔ cup vegetable oil or peanut oil

3 ounces dried rice vermicelli noodles

2 shallots, thinly sliced

2 garlic cloves, crushed

1-inch piece fresh ginger, thinly sliced

8 ounces tenderloin steak, cut into thin strips

2 tablespoons Thai green curry paste

2 tablespoons Thai soy sauce

1 tablespoon Thai fish sauce

fresh cilantro, to garnish

1. Pour the stock into a large saucepan and bring to a boil. Meanwhile, preheat a wok or large skillet over high heat. Add the oil and heat until hot. Add one-third of the noodles to the wok and cook, stirring, for 10–20 seconds, until puffed up. Lift out with tongs, drain on paper towels, and set aside. Pour off all but 2 tablespoons of the oil from the wok.

2. Add the shallots, garlic, and ginger to the wok and stir-fry for 1 minute. Add the beef and curry paste and stir-fry for 3–4 minutes, until tender.

3. Transfer the beef mixture to the saucepan of stock with the uncooked noodles, soy sauce, and fish sauce. Simmer for 2–3 minutes, until the noodles have swelled.

4. Transfer the soup to warm serving bowls. Garnish with cilantro and serve immediately topped with the crispy noodles.

Chicken & Summer Vegetable Soup

 SERVES 4    PREP TIME: 10 minutes    COOKING TIME: 15–20 minutes

nutritional information per serving	228 cal, 8g fat, 1g sat fat, 5g total sugars, 0.8g salt

This light, fresh-tasting chicken soup will become a favorite.

INGREDIENTS

2 tablespoons olive oil

2 skinless, boneless chicken breasts, thinly sliced

2 garlic cloves, crushed

2 zucchini, cut into ½-inch dice

2 cups cut green beans (½-inch pieces)

3 tomatoes, seeded and coarsely chopped

1 (15-ounce) can pinto beans or cranberry beans, drained and rinsed

5 cups vegetable stock

12 fresh basil leaves, torn into pieces

pepper

fresh Parmesan cheese shavings, to serve

1. Heat the oil in a large saucepan over medium heat. Add the chicken and garlic and cook, stirring, for 3 minutes. Try not to let the chicken or garlic brown.

2. Stir in the zucchini, green beans, tomatoes, pinto beans, and stock. Cover and simmer for 10–12 minutes, or until the chicken is cooked all the way through. Stir in the basil leaves and season with pepper.

3. Transfer the soup to warm serving bowls. Serve immediately with Parmesan cheese shavings.

Chili Beef Stir-Fry

 SERVES 4    PREP TIME: 10 minutes    COOKING TIME: 7 minutes

nutritional information
per serving   331 cal, 18g fat, 4g sat fat, 4g total sugars, 1.3g salt

Set the table before you start to cook this flavorful stir-fry, then eat right away.

INGREDIENTS

1 pound top sirloin steak, cut into thin strips

1 ripe avocado

10 cherry tomatoes

2 tablespoons sunflower oil

1 (15-ounce) can red kidney beans, drained and rinsed

chopped fresh cilantro, to garnish

tortilla chips and shredded iceberg lettuce, to serve

marinade

2 garlic cloves, crushed

1 teaspoon chili powder

½ teaspoon salt

1 teaspoon ground coriander

1. For the marinade, put the garlic, chili powder, salt, and ground coriander in a large bowl and stir until well mixed.

2. Add the strips of beef to the marinade and toss thoroughly to coat all over.

3. Using a sharp knife, peel the avocado. Slice lengthwise in half and remove and discard the pit, then slice crosswise to form small dice. Halve the cherry tomatoes.

4. Preheat a wok or large skillet over high heat. Add the oil and heat until hot. Add the beef and stir-fry for 5 minutes, tossing frequently. Add the kidney beans, tomatoes, and avocado and cook for 2 minutes.

5. Transfer the salad to a serving bowl. Garnish with cilantro and serve immediately with tortilla chips and lettuce.

2

3

4

COOK'S NOTE
A nonstick wok is a great piece of kitchen equipment to have, and you will find it useful in a wide variety of recipes. After use, wipe the inside of the wok well with paper towels to remove grease and stuck-on food.

Bacon, Lettuce & Tomato Salad

 SERVES 4    PREP TIME: 10 minutes    COOKING TIME: 5 minutes

nutritional information per serving : 336 cal, 30g fat, 8g sat fat, 3g total sugars, 3.2g salt

This is the classic combo of bacon, lettuce, and tomato—and don't forget the dressing!

INGREDIENTS

8 thick bacon strips

½ ripe avocado, peeled, pitted, and sliced

1 tablespoon lemon juice

1 iceberg lettuce, cut into 12 wedges

2 beefsteak tomatoes, sliced into wedges

¼ cucumber, thickly sliced

dressing

¼ cup mayonnaise

2 tablespoons sour cream

1 tablespoon milk

2 teaspoons whole-grain mustard

salt and pepper

1. Preheat the broiler to high. Place the bacon strips on the broiler pan and broil for 3–4 minutes, turning once, until crisp.

2. To make the dressing, put the mayonnaise, sour cream, milk, and mustard in a bowl and beat together until smooth. Season with salt and pepper.

3. Toss the avocado slices in the lemon juice. Divide the lettuce, tomatoes, cucumber, and avocado among serving plates. Add the bacon strips, pour the dressing over the salad, and serve immediately.

1
2
3

COOK'S NOTE
To remove the ripe avocado quickly from its skin, halve and remove the pit. Slide a tablespoon into the flesh at the wide end, scooping down to the point. The flesh will come out whole for you to slice or chop.

Honey & Chicken Pasta Salad

 SERVES 4

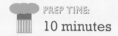 PREP TIME:
10 minutes

 COOKING TIME:
15 minutes

nutritional information per serving	517 cal, 17g fat, 2.5g sat fat, 14.5g total sugars, 0.7g salt

Have a selection of pasta shapes among your staples so that you can quickly assemble a great recipe such as this.

INGREDIENTS

8 ounces dried fusilli

2 tablespoons olive oil

1 onion, thinly sliced

1 garlic clove, crushed

1 pound skinless, boneless chicken breasts, thinly sliced

2 tablespoons whole-grain mustard

2 tablespoons honey

10 cherry tomatoes, halved

handful of fresh arugula

fresh thyme leaves, to garnish

salt

dressing

3 tablespoons olive oil

1 tablespoon sherry vinegar

2 teaspoons honey

1 tablespoon fresh thyme leaves

salt and pepper

1. To make the dressing, put all the ingredients in a small bowl and beat together.

2. Bring a large saucepan of lightly salted water to a boil. Add the pasta, bring back to a boil, and cook according to the package directions, until tender but still firm to the bite.

3. Heat the oil in a large saucepan over medium heat. Add the onion, garlic, and chicken and cook, stirring frequently, for 3–4 minutes, or until the chicken is cooked all the way through. Stir the mustard and honey into the pan and cook for an additional 2–3 minutes.

4. Drain the pasta and transfer to a serving bowl. Pour the dressing over the pasta and toss well. Stir in the chicken and onion and let cool. Gently stir the tomatoes and arugula into the pasta.

5. Transfer to warm serving plates, garnish with thyme, and serve immediately.

Lentil & Tuna Salad

 SERVES 4    PREP TIME: 15 minutes   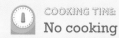 COOKING TIME: No cooking

nutritional information per serving   234 cal, 9g fat, 1.5g sat fat, 3.5g total sugars, 0.4g salt

The delicious dressing for this salad turns canned tuna and lentils into something special.

INGREDIENTS

2 ripe tomatoes

1 small red onion

1 (15½-ounce) can lentils, drained

1 (5-ounce) can solid white tuna in water, drained

2 tablespoons chopped fresh cilantro

pepper

dressing

3 tablespoons virgin olive oil

1 tablespoon lemon juice

1 teaspoon whole-grain mustard

1 garlic clove, crushed

½ teaspoon ground cumin

½ teaspoon ground coriander

1. Using a sharp knife, seed the tomatoes and chop them into small dice. Finely chop the red onion.

2. To make the dressing, beat all ingredients in a small bowl until thoroughly combined. Set aside until required.

3. Mix together the chopped onion, diced tomatoes, and drained lentils in a large bowl.

4. Flake the tuna with a fork and stir it into the lentil mixture. Stir in the cilantro and mix well.

5. Pour the dressing over the salad and season with pepper. Serve immediately.

1

1

4

COOK'S NOTE *Have the dressing already prepared in screw-top jars in the refrigerator.*

Tomato, Olive & Mozzarella
Pasta Salad

 SERVES 4    PREP TIME: 5 minutes    COOKING TIME: 10 minutes

nutritional information
per serving — 593 cal, 35g fat, 10g sat fat, 9g total sugars, 0.7g salt

Conchiglie are shell-shaped pasta that work particularly well in salads; however, you can use whatever pasta shapes you have in the pantry.

INGREDIENTS

8 ounces dried conchiglie

⅓ cup pine nuts

2½ cups halved cherry tomatoes

1 red bell pepper, seeded and cut into bite-size chunks

1 red onion, chopped

8 ounces mozzarella, cut into small pieces

12 ripe black olives, pitted

1 cup fresh basil leaves

fresh Parmesan cheese shavings, to garnish

salt

dressing
⅓ cup extra-virgin olive oil

2 tablespoons balsamic vinegar

1 tablespoon chopped fresh basil

salt and pepper

1. Bring a large saucepan of lightly salted water to a boil. Add the pasta, bring back to a boil, and cook according to the package directions, until tender but still firm to the bite. Drain, refresh under cold running water, and drain again. Let cool.

2. Meanwhile, heat a dry skillet over low heat, add the pine nuts, and cook, shaking the skillet frequently, for 1–2 minutes, until lightly toasted. Remove from the heat, transfer to a dish, and let cool.

3. To make the dressing, put all the ingredients in a small bowl and mix together well. Cover with plastic wrap and set aside.

4. Divide the pasta among serving bowls. Add the pine nuts, tomatoes, pepper, onion, mozzarella, and olives to each bowl. Sprinkle with the basil, then drizzle with the dressing. Garnish with Parmesan cheese shavings and serve immediately.

Avocado Salad with Lime Dressing

 SERVES 4

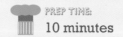 PREP TIME:
10 minutes

 COOKING TIME:
No cooking

nutritional information
per serving | 300 cal, 28g fat, 5g sat fat, 6g total sugars, 0.1g salt

The wonderful combination of flavors and textures in this salad are tossed in a tangy dressing flavored with mustard.

INGREDIENTS

2¼ cups mixed red and
green lettuce

3 cups wild arugula

4 scallions, finely diced

5 tomatoes, sliced

¼ cup toasted and
chopped walnuts

2 avocados

1 tablespoon lemon juice

lime dressing

1 tablespoon lime juice

1 teaspoon French mustard

1 tablespoon sour cream

1 tablespoon chopped fresh
parsley or cilantro

3 tablespoons extra-virgin
olive oil

pinch of sugar

salt and pepper

1. Tear the lettuce and arrange with arugula in the bottom of a large salad bowl. Add the scallions, tomatoes, and walnuts.

2. Using a sharp knife, peel the avocado. Slice the avocado lengthwise in half and remove and discard the pit, then slice crosswise. Brush with the lemon juice to prevent discoloration, then transfer the flesh to the salad bowl. Gently mix together.

3. To make the dressing, put all the dressing ingredients in a screw-top jar and shake well. Drizzle the dressing over the salad and serve immediately.

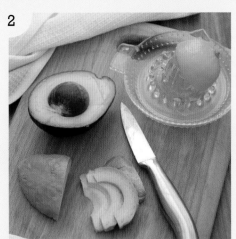

Cheese Steak Baguette

🍴 SERVES 4   👨‍🍳 PREP TIME: 5 minutes   ⏲ COOKING TIME: 15–20 minutes

nutritional information per serving	540 cal, 20g fat, 7g sat fat, 6g total sugars, 2.1g salt

Whether you call this American classic a "hoagie," "sub," or "hero," you'll love it.

INGREDIENTS

1 baguette

12 ounces boneless rib-eye steak, partially frozen

3 tablespoons olive oil

1 onion, thinly sliced

1 green bell pepper, cored, seeded, and thinly sliced

salt and pepper

3 ounces halloumi or mozzarella cheese, thinly sliced

1. Cut the baguette into four equal lengths, then cut each piece in half horizontally. Thinly slice the partially frozen steak across the grain.

2. Heat 2 tablespoons of the oil in a large skillet over medium heat, add the onion and bell pepper, and cook, stirring occasionally, for 10–15 minutes, until both vegetables are softened and the onion is golden brown. Push the mixture to one side of the skillet.

3. Heat the remaining oil in the skillet over medium heat. When hot, add the steak and stir-fry for 4–5 minutes, until tender. Stir the onion mixture and steak together and season with salt and pepper.

4. Preheat the broiler to medium. Divide the steak mixture among the four bottom halves of bread and top with the cheese. Place them on a broiler rack and broil for 1–2 minutes, until the cheese has melted, then cover with the top halves of bread and press down gently to serve.

1

2

3

Meatball Sub

 SERVES 4   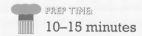 PREP TIME: 10–15 minutes   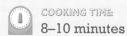 COOKING TIME: 8–10 minutes

nutritional information per serving	490 cal, 19g fat, 6g sat fat, 4.8g total sugars, 1.5g salt

For a really tasty quick lunch, this meaty submarine will satisfy even the heartiest of appetites.

INGREDIENTS

1 pound lean ground beef
1 onion, grated
1 garlic clove, crushed
2 teaspoon mild chili powder
½ cup fresh whole-wheat bread crumbs
oil, for pan-frying
salt and pepper

to serve
lettuce
4 sub rolls, halved lengthwise
1 red onion, thinly sliced into rings

1. Place the meat in a large mixing bowl. Add the onion, garlic, chili powder, and bread crumbs. Season with salt and pepper and mix together. Use a small ice-cream scoop to shape the mixture into small balls.

2. Heat a shallow depth of oil in a deep skillet until hot. Add the meatballs, in batches, and cook for 8–10 minutes, until cooked all the way through.

3. Lift out the meatballs with a slotted spoon and drain on absorbent paper towels.

4. Place the lettuce on the bottom halves of the rolls and top with the meatballs. Place the onion rings on top, cover with the lids, and serve immediately.

1

1

2

SOMETHING DIFFERENT

Try adding 1 teaspoon of hot chili sauce to the ingredients in step 1 for a spicier meatball.

Paprika Steak Wraps with Horseradish Cream

🍴 SERVES 4

👨‍🍳 PREP TIME:
5 minutes

⏱ COOKING TIME:
10–15 minutes

nutritional information
per serving   826 cal, 42g fat, 17g sat fat, 4g total sugars, 1.9g salt

Tortillas or wraps are definitely something to have on hand for a "sandwich" that's made in a flash.

INGREDIENTS

4 tenderloin steaks, about 1 pound each

1 garlic clove, crushed

2 teaspoon smoked paprika, plus extra for sprinkling

sunflower oil, for brushing

½ cup crème fraîche or sour cream

3 tablespoons creamed horseradish

8 small flour tortillas

4 cups arugula

2 ripe avocados, peeled, pitted, and sliced

1 red onion, thinly sliced

salt and pepper

1. Spread the steaks with the garlic and sprinkle both sides with the paprika. Season with salt and pepper.

2. Preheat a ridged grill pan to hot and brush with oil. Add the steaks and cook for 6–8 minutes, turning once. Remove from the heat and let rest for 5 minutes.

3. Meanwhile, put the créme fraîche and horseradish in a small bowl and mix together. Spread half the mixture over each tortilla.

4. Slice the steaks into strips. Divide among the tortillas with the arugula, avocado, and red onion, wrapping the sides over. Serve immediately with a spoonful of horseradish cream, sprinkled with extra paprika.

SOMETHING DIFFERENT
If horseradish cream is not to your taste, use a store-bought spicy salsa in the tortilla wrap instead.

Smoked Chicken & Ham Focaccia

 SERVES 4    PREP TIME: 10 minutes    COOKING TIME: 5 minutes

nutritional information per serving	533 cal, 22g fat, 11.5g sat fat, 2g total sugars, 2.7g salt

Focaccia is a traditional Italian bread that we've taken to our hearts. It's the perfect choice for a chunky toasted sandwich.

INGREDIENTS

1 thick focaccia loaf
2 small zucchini
handful of fresh basil leaves
6 wafer-thin smoked chicken slices
6 wafer-thin cooked ham slices
8 ounces Taleggio cheese or Monterey Jack cheese, cut into strips
freshly grated nutmeg (optional)
cherry tomatoes and lettuce, to serve

1. Preheat a griddle plate or pan under the broiler until both the broiler and griddle are hot. Slice the focaccia in half horizontally and cut the top half lengthwise into strips.

2. Coarsely shred the zucchini using a grater. Cover the bottom half of the focaccia with the zucchini, top with basil leaves, and cover with the chicken and ham. Lay the strips of focaccia on top, placing strips of cheese between them. Sprinkle with a little nutmeg, if using.

3. Place the assembled bread on the hot griddle and cook under the preheated broiler, well away from the heat, for about 5 minutes, until the cheese has melted and the top of the bread is browned. Cut the focaccia into four pieces and serve immediately with cherry tomatoes and lettuce.

2
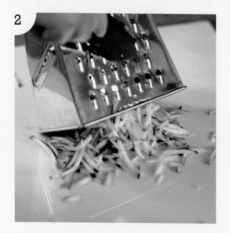

2

3

Turkey Wraps with Brie & Cranberry

 SERVES 4

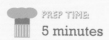 PREP TIME:
5 minutes

 COOKING TIME:
1 minute

nutritional information per serving	424 cal, 16g fat, 9.5g sat fat, 5g total sugars, 1.4g salt

Although an ideal recipe for after Christmas to use up leftover turkey and cranberry sauce, you may find yourself craving the flavor combination at other times of the year. Use cooked chicken if you prefer.

INGREDIENTS

4 flour tortillas
¼ cup cranberry sauce
2 cups shredded, cooked turkey breast
5 ounces brie, sliced
salt and pepper

1. Preheat a nonstick pan or griddle pan until almost smoking, then cook the tortillas one at a time on each side for 10 seconds.

2. Spread the cranberry sauce over the tortillas. Divide the turkey and brie among the tortillas and season with salt and pepper. Wrap the sides over and serve immediately.

GOES WELL
WITH
Serve with a
green salad for
a quick lunch
or light dinner.

Hot Salmon, Tomato & Cream Cheese on a Bagel

 SERVES 2

 PREP TIME: 5 minutes

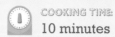 COOKING TIME: 10 minutes

nutritional information **per serving** — 500 cal, 27g fat, 11g sat fat, 8g total sugars, 3.4g salt

For a change of pace, choose a flavored bagel such as a sesame seed bagel or onion bagel.

INGREDIENTS

2 bagels

2 tomatoes, thinly sliced

grated zest of 1 lemon

1 scallion, chopped

1 tablespoon olive oil

4 slices smoked salmon (about 4 ounces)

¼ cup cream cheese

pepper

lemon wedges, to serve

1. Preheat the broiler to medium–high. Slice the bagels in half horizontally and place them, cut sides down, on the rack in the broiler pan. Toast until browned, then turn over.

2. Cover the bottom halves of the bagels with tomato slices. Sprinkle with lemon zest and scallion, then season with pepper. Drizzle the olive oil over the tomatoes and broil for 1–2 minutes, until the tomatoes are lightly cooked.

3. Arrange the smoked salmon slices on the tomatoes, wrinkling them slightly, and return them under the broiler for a minute to cook the salmon lightly and brown the edges in places.

4. Top each with a spoonful of cream cheese and add the toasted bagel lids. Serve immediately with lemon wedges.

Mini Muffin Pizzas

 SERVES 2

 PREP TIME:
10 minutes

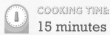 COOKING TIME:
15 minutes

nutritional information per serving	643 cal, 35g fat, 13g sat fat, 8g total sugars, 2.9g salt

Children will love these quick 'n' easy mini pizzas, and they can do the assembling with a little supervision. They make great after-school treats.

INGREDIENTS

3 whole-wheat English muffins, halved

2 tablespoons tomato paste

2 tablespoons pesto

1 tablespoon olive oil

½ red onion, thinly sliced

3 mushrooms, sliced

½ zucchini, thinly sliced

2–3 slices cooked ham

1 cup shredded cheddar cheese

cherry tomatoes, to serve

1. Toast the muffins until golden, then let cool.

2. Mix the tomato paste and pesto in a small bowl and spread equally over the muffin halves.

3. Heat the oil in a large saucepan over medium heat. Add the onion, mushrooms, and zucchini and cook until soft and beginning to brown.

4. Preheat the broiler to high. Divide the vegetables among the muffins and top with the ham and then the cheese. Cook under the preheated broiler for 3–4 minutes, until the cheese has melted and browned. Serve immediately with cherry tomatoes.

2

3

4

BE PREPARED
Make earlier in the day, place on a baking sheet, and cover with plastic wrap. Refrigerate until required. Heat the broiler, remove the plastic wrap, and cook.

Roasted Vegetable & Feta Cheese Wraps

 SERVES 4

 PREP TIME:
10 minutes

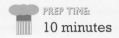 COOKING TIME:
20–25 minutes

nutritional information per serving | 374 cal, 20g fat, 7g sat fat, 5g total sugars, 1.7g salt

Roasting the vegetables brings out their natural sweetness, which caramelizes and combines perfectly with the tangy feta cheese.

INGREDIENTS

1 red onion, cut into eighths

1 red bell pepper, cored and cut into eighths

1 small eggplant, cut into eighths

1 zucchini, cut into eighths

¼ cup extra-virgin olive oil

1 garlic clove, crushed

⅔ cup crumbled feta cheese

small bunch of fresh mint, shredded

4 flour tortillas

salt and pepper

1. Preheat the oven to 425°F. Mix the vegetables, olive oil, and garlic in a nonstick baking pan and season with salt and pepper. Roast for 15–20 minutes in the preheated oven, or until golden and cooked all the way through.

2. Remove from the oven and cool. Mix in the feta and mint.

3. Preheat a nonstick skillet or ridged grill pan until almost smoking. Add the tortillas and warm for a few seconds. Remove from the skillet.

4. Divide the vegetable and feta mixture among the tortillas. Fold the sides over and serve immediately.

1

2

4

SOMETHING
DIFFERENT
Spread the
tortillas with a
little store-bought
hummus or tahini
dressing before
topping with the
roasted vegetables
and cheese.

Spicy Beef Nachos 70

Thai Beef 72

Hot Sesame Beef 74

Beef Chop Suey 76

Sliced Beef in Black Bean Sauce 78

Teriyaki Steak 80

Sliced Steak with Tomato & Red Pepper Salsa 82

Quick Spaghetti with Meat Sauce 84

Quick Chili con Carne 86

Beef Fajitas 88

Classic Hamburgers 90

Orange & Lemon Crispy Lamb Cutlets 92

Honeyed Apricot Lamb with Lemon Couscous 94

Herbed Lamb Burgers 96

Pork in Plum Sauce 98

Pork Pad Thai 100

Spicy Pork Meatballs 102

Pepperoni Pasta 104

Creamy Bolognese Pasta 106

Spaghetti with Bacon & Crispy Bread Crumbs 108

Chorizo & Chickpea Casserole 110

Pork & Rosemary Burgers 112

Prosciutto & Red Pepper Pizza 114

Meat

Spicy Beef Nachos

 SERVES 4  PREP TIME: 5 minutes  COOKING TIME: 10–12 minutes

nutritional information per serving	540 cal, 37g fat, 15g sat fat, 5g total sugars, 1.4g salt

Super-fast to prepare, this dish is also super-easy to eat—just grab a fork—perfect to enjoy while watching TV.

INGREDIENTS

1 tablespoon sunflower oil

1 red onion, sliced

1 pound lean ground beef

1 garlic clove, crushed

1½ teaspoons crushed red pepper

4 tomatoes, diced

1 avocado, peeled and diced

3 ounces tortilla chips, coarsely broken up

1⅓ cups shredded cheddar cheese

salt and pepper

1. Heat the oil in a large skillet over medium heat. Add the onion and ground beef and sauté, stirring, for 6–8 minutes.

2. Stir in the garlic, crushed red pepper, and tomatoes and cook for an additional 2 minutes. Season well with salt and pepper.

3. Preheat the broiler to medium–high. Transfer the meat to an oven-proof dish. Scatter the avocado and tortilla chips over the dish and sprinkle with grated cheese.

4. Cook the nachos under the preheated broiler for 2 minutes, until the cheese is melted. Serve immediately.

GOES WELL
WITH
A large crisp salad
of romaine lettuce
and cucumber and
a spoonful of sour
cream make a cooling
accompaniment.

Thai Beef

 SERVES 4   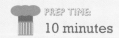 PREP TIME: 10 minutes    COOKING TIME: 15–20 minutes

nutritional information
per serving | 407 cal, 28g fat, 18g sat fat, 6g total sugars, 0.5g salt

The tender steak, stir-fried with crispy broccoli, has coconut milk and fresh herbs stirred in at the end of cooking.

INGREDIENTS

2 tablespoons vegetable oil

2 tablespoons Thai green curry paste

2 tenderloin steaks (about 6 ounces each), thinly sliced

2 onions, sliced

6 scallions, chopped

2 shallots, finely chopped

3 cups broccoli florets

1¾ cups coconut milk

3 kaffir lime leaves, coarsely chopped

¼ cup chopped fresh cilantro

handful of Thai basil leaves

1. Preheat a wok or large skillet over high heat. Add the oil and heat until hot. Add the curry paste and stir-fry for 1–2 minutes. Add the beef, in batches, if necessary, and stir-fry until starting to brown.

2. Add the onions, scallions, and shallots and stir-fry for 2–3 minutes. Add the broccoli and stir-fry for 2–3 minutes. Pour in the coconut milk, add the lime leaves, and bring to a boil.

3. Simmer gently for 8–10 minutes, until the meat is tender. Stir in the cilantro and basil.

4. Transfer to warm serving bowls and serve immediately.

Hot Sesame Beef

 SERVES 4   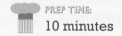 PREP TIME: 10 minutes    COOKING TIME: 10–12 minutes

nutritional information per serving	553 cal, 24g fat, 6g sat fat, 5g total sugars, 1.8g salt

What could be easier than this spicy beef stir-fry flavored with chili and sesame seeds and served on aromatic basmati rice?

INGREDIENTS

1 cup long-grain rice

1 pound tenderloin steak, cut into thin strips

1½ tablespoons sesame seeds

½ cup beef stock

2 tablespoons soy sauce

2 tablespoons grated fresh ginger

2 garlic cloves, finely chopped

1 teaspoon cornstarch

½ teaspoon crushed red pepper

3 tablespoons sesame oil

1 large head of broccoli, cut into florets

1 yellow bell pepper, seeded and thinly sliced

1 fresh red chile, finely sliced

1 tablespoon chili oil, or to taste

salt and pepper

1 tablespoon chopped fresh cilantro, to garnish

1. Cook the rice in a saucepan of lightly salted water, until tender according to the package directions. Drain.

2. Meanwhile, place the beef strips and 1 tablespoon of the sesame seeds in a bowl and mix together.

3. Put the stock, soy sauce, ginger, garlic, cornstarch, and crushed red pepper in a separate bowl and mix together.

4. Preheat a wok or large skillet over high heat. Add 1 tablespoon of the sesame oil and heat until hot. Add the beef and stir-fry until starting to brown. Remove and set aside, then wipe the wok with paper towels.

5. Heat the remaining sesame oil in the wok, add the broccoli, yellow bell pepper, red chile, and chili oil, and stir-fry for 2–3 minutes. Stir in the stock mixture, cover, and simmer for 2 minutes.

6. Return the beef to the wok and simmer until the juices thicken, stirring occasionally. Cook for an additional 1–2 minutes. Sprinkle with the remaining sesame seeds and season with salt and pepper.

7. Transfer the rice to warm serving bowls and top with the beef and vegetables. Garnish with chopped cilantro and serve immediately.

Beef Chop Suey

 SERVES 4    PREP TIME: 5 minutes plus marinating    COOKING TIME: 5 minutes

nutritional information per serving	290 cal, 12.5g fat, 3g sat fat, 6g total sugars, 3g salt

Chinese rice wine is used a lot in Chinese cooking, but dry sherry is a good substitute.

INGREDIENTS

1 pound rib-eye steak, sliced

1 head of broccoli, cut into florets

2 tablespoons vegetable oil

1 onion, sliced

2 celery stalks, sliced

3 cups snow peas (sliced lengthwise)

⅓ cup rinsed and shredded canned bamboo shoots

8 water chestnuts, sliced

3 cups sliced white button mushrooms

1 tablespoon oyster sauce

1 teaspoon salt

marinade

1 tablespoon Chinese rice wine

½ teaspoon white pepper

½ teaspoon salt

1 tablespoon light soy sauce

½ teaspoon sesame oil

1. Put all the marinade ingredients in a bowl and mix together. Add the beef and marinate for at least 20 minutes.

2. Blanch the broccoli in a large saucepan of boiling water for 30 seconds. Drain and set aside.

3. Preheat a wok or large skillet over high heat. Add 1 tablespoon of the oil and heat until hot. Add the beef and stir-fry until starting to brown. Remove and set aside, then wipe the wok with paper towels.

4. Heat the remaining oil and stir-fry the onion for 1 minute. Add the celery and broccoli and cook for 2 minutes. Add the snow peas, bamboo shoots, water chestnuts, and mushrooms and cook for 1 minute. Add the beef and oyster sauce and season with salt.

5. Transfer to warm serving bowls and serve immediately.

Sliced Beef in Black Bean Sauce

 SERVES 4    PREP TIME: 5 minutes   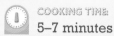 COOKING TIME: 5–7 minutes

nutritional information per serving	270 cal, 14g fat, 4g sat fat, 7g total sugars, 1.4g salt

Chinese-style black bean sauce can be found in the Asian sections of supermarkets. You can make your own, but keeping a jar in the refrigerator saves time.

INGREDIENTS

3 tablespoons peanut oil

1 pound tenderloin steak, thinly sliced

1 red bell pepper, seeded and thinly sliced

1 green bell pepper, seeded and thinly sliced

1 bunch scallions, sliced

2 garlic cloves, crushed

1 tablespoon grated fresh ginger

2 tablespoons black bean sauce

1 tablespoon sherry

1 tablespoon soy sauce

1. Preheat a wok or large skillet over high heat. Add 2 tablespoons of the oil and heat until hot. Add the beef and stir-fry until starting to brown. Remove and set aside.

2. Add the remaining oil and bell peppers and stir-fry for 2 minutes.

3. Add the scallions, garlic, and ginger and stir-fry for 30 seconds.

4. Add the black bean sauce, sherry, and soy sauce, then stir in the beef and heat until bubbling.

5. Transfer to warm serving bowls and serve immediately.

1

2

3

COOK'S NOTE
To slice beef thinly,
first freeze it,
wrapped in plastic
wrap, for 30 minutes.
Using a sharp knife
helps, too.

Teriyaki Steak

 SERVES 4   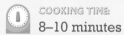 PREP TIME: 10 minutes    COOKING TIME: 8–10 minutes

nutritional information
per serving   284 cal, 12g fat, 3g sat fat, 4g total sugars, 2.9g salt

Teriyaki is a Japanese method of cooking meat, fish, or poultry in a skillet or under a broiler with a sweet sauce.

INGREDIENTS

4 tenderloin steaks, about
5 ounces each

2 tablespoons vegetable oil

2 cups fresh bean sprouts

4 scallions, trimmed
and finely sliced

salt and pepper

teriyaki sauce
2 tablespoons mirin
(Japanese rice wine)

2 tablespoons sake
or pale dry sherry

4 tbsp dark soy sauce

1 tsp granulated sugar

1. Season the steaks with salt and pepper and set aside. To make the sauce, put the mirin, sake, soy sauce, and sugar in a bowl and mix together.

2. Meanwhile, preheat a large skillet over high heat. Add 1 tablespoon of oil and heat until hot. Add the bean sprouts and sauté quickly, tossing in the hot oil for 30 seconds. Remove from the skillet and drain on paper towels.

3. Add the remaining oil to the skillet and heat until hot. Add the steaks and cook for 3–5 minutes on each side, or until cooked to your liking. Remove from the skillet and keep warm.

4. Remove the skillet from the heat and add the sauce and scallions. Return to the heat and simmer for 2 minutes, stirring until the sauce thickens slightly and is glossy.

5. Transfer the bean sprouts to warm serving plates, slice each steak, and arrange on top. Spoon the sauce over and serve immediately.

1

2

3

COOK'S NOTE Fresh bean sprouts spoil quickly, so use them as soon as you can.

Sliced Steak with a Tomato & Red Pepper Salsa

SERVES 4

PREP TIME:
6 minutes

COOKING TIME:
8 minutes

nutritional information per serving	255 cal, 12g fat, 3.5g sat fat, 5g total sugars, 0.2g salt

A fresh, colorful salsa is the ideal partner for a really good steak, and it's made in minutes!

INGREDIENTS

1 pound tenderloin steak
olive oil, for brushing
salt and pepper
crusty bread, to serve

salsa
2 tomatoes, quartered
1 red bell pepper, seeded and cut into chunks
1 small red onion, quartered
1 small garlic clove, chopped
2 tablespoons olive oil
1 tablespoon red-wine vinegar
3 tablespoons chopped fresh cilantro
salt and pepper

1. To make the salsa, put the tomatoes, red bell pepper, onion, and garlic in a food processor and pulse for a few seconds, until coarsely chopped. Stir in the oil, vinegar, and cilantro. Season with salt and pepper. Cover and let marinate at room temperature.

2. Meanwhile, preheat a large skillet over high heat. Season the steaks with salt and pepper and brush with oil. Place the steak in the hot skillet and cook for 2–5 minutes on each side, or until cooked to your liking. Remove from the skillet and keep warm.

3. Slice the steaks into strips. Transfer to warm serving plates and serve immediately with the salsa and slices of crusty bread.

Quick Spaghetti with Meat Sauce

 SERVES 4  PREP TIME: 5 minutes 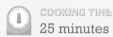 COOKING TIME: 25 minutes

nutritional information **per serving** — 508 cal, 18g fat, 6g sat fat, 9g total sugars, 0.5g salt

This is a speedy version of a family favorite that originated in Bologna, Italy.

INGREDIENTS

8 ounces spaghetti
mixed salad, to serve

meat sauce
2 tablespoons olive oil
1 large onion, chopped
1 pound lean ground beef
1 green bell pepper, seeded and chopped
1 garlic clove, crushed
⅔ cup red wine
1 (14½-ounce) can diced tomatoes
2 tablespoons tomato paste
1 tablespoon dried oregano
salt and pepper

1. Heat the oil in a large saucepan over high heat, add the onion and ground beef, and sauté, stirring, until lightly browned.

2. Stir in the green bell pepper and garlic, then add the wine, tomatoes, tomato paste, and oregano. Season with salt and pepper. Bring to a boil and boil rapidly for 2 minutes. Reduce the heat, cover, and simmer for 20 minutes, stirring occasionally.

3. Meanwhile, bring a large saucepan of lightly salted water to a boil. Add the spaghetti, bring back to a boil, and cook according to the package directions, until tender but still firm to the bite. Drain.

4. Stir the meat sauce into the spaghetti. Transfer to warm serving bowls and serve immediately with a mixed salad.

SOMETHING DIFFERENT
To enrich the flavor of the sauce, finely chop 2 strips of smoked bacon or pancetta and sauté with the ground beef in step 1.

Quick Chili con Carne

 SERVES 4    PREP TIME: 15 minutes   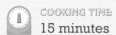 COOKING TIME: 15 minutes

nutritional information per serving	551 cal, 18.5g fat, 6g sat fat, 8.5g total sugars, 1.5g salt

A bowl of chili is perfect for feeding a crowd, for parties, or a family feast.

INGREDIENTS

1 cup long-grain rice

2 tablespoons olive oil

1 large onion, sliced

1 pound lean ground beef

1 garlic clove, crushed

1 (14½-ounce) can diced tomatoes

1 (15-ounce) can red kidney beans, drained

1 cup beef stock

2 tablespoons tomato paste

2 teaspoons crushed red pepper

salt and pepper

crusty bread, to serve

1. Cook the rice in a saucepan of lightly salted water according to the package directions, until tender. Drain.

2. Meanwhile, heat the oil in a large saucepan over high heat, add the onion and ground beef, and sauté, stirring, until lightly browned.

3. Stir in the garlic, then add the tomatoes, beans, stock, tomato paste, and crushed red pepper. Season with salt and pepper. Stir until boiling, then reduce the heat, cover, and simmer for 15 minutes, stirring occasionally.

4. Transfer to warm serving bowls and serve immediately with the rice and crusty bread.

2

3

3

Beef Fajitas

🍴 SERVES 4   👨‍🍳 PREP TIME: 10 minutes   ⏲ COOKING TIME: 4–6 minutes

nutritional information per serving	500 cal, 23g fat, 9g sat fat, 4g total sugars, 0.8g salt

"Fajita" comes from the Spanish for "belt" or "girdle," referring to the skirt steak traditionally used for the dish.

INGREDIENTS

1 pound skirt steak
1 garlic clove, halved
olive oil, for brushing
4 large wheat tortillas
⅔ cup sour cream
salt and pepper

guacamole

1 large ripe avocado
juice of ½ lime
1 teaspoon hot chili sauce
1 small red onion, diced
1 tomato, chopped
1 tablespoon chopped
fresh cilantro
salt and pepper

1. To make the guacamole, use a sharp knife to peel the avocado. Slice the avocado lengthwise in half and remove and discard the pit. Mash with the lime juice. Add the chili sauce, onion, tomato, and cilantro. Season with salt and pepper.

2. Rub the steak with the garlic, season with salt and pepper, and brush with oil. Heat a heavy skillet or griddle pan until hot.

3. Add the steak to the skillet and cook for 1–3 minutes on each side, or until cooked to your liking. Remove from the skillet and keep warm.

4. Add the tortillas to the skillet and warm for a few seconds. Remove from the skillet.

5. Slice the steak and divide it among the tortillas. Add a spoonful of guacamole and sour cream to each. Fold up the sides and serve immediately.

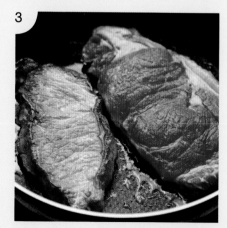

Classic Hamburgers

 SERVES 4    PREP TIME: 10 minutes   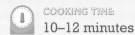 COOKING TIME: 10–12 minutes

nutritional information per serving	715 cal, 40g fat, 17g sat fat, 3.5g total sugars, 2.4g salt

You can't beat a homemade hamburger. Ours come with a sprinkling of cheese.

INGREDIENTS

1½ pounds fresh ground beef

1 beef bouillon cube

2 tablespoons chopped fresh basil, plus a few sprigs to garnish

2 tablespoons water

½ cup shredded American cheese or cheddar cheese

to serve

4 hamburger buns, halved

mustard

ketchup

1. Preheat the broiler to medium–high. Place the beef in a large mixing bowl. Crumble the bouillon cube over the beef, add the chopped basil and water, and mix well.

2. Divide the meat into four portions, shape each into a ball, then flatten slightly to make a patty shape of your preferred thickness.

3. Cook the burgers under the preheated grill for 5–6 minutes. Turn the burgers, sprinkle cheese over the cooked side, and cook for an additional 5–6 minutes, until cooked all the way through.

4. Place the burgers on the bottom halves of the buns and top with the lids. Garnish with sprigs of basil and serve immediately with mustard and ketchup.

Orange & Lemon Crispy Lamb Cutlets

 SERVES 2    PREP TIME: 5 minutes   COOKING TIME: 8–10 minutes

nutritional information per serving	355 cal, 22g fat, 8g sat fat, 0g total sugars, 0.4g salt

Tender lamb cutlets brushed with a garlic-citrus glaze will smell delicious as they cook and taste even better. Trimming the bones before cooking makes them easy to pick up with your fingers.

INGREDIENTS

1 garlic clove, crushed

1 tablespoon olive oil

2 tablespoons finely grated orange rind

2 tablespoons finely grated lemon rind

6 lamb cutlets

salt and pepper

orange wedges, to garnish

1. Put the garlic, oil, and citrus rinds in a bowl. Season with salt and pepper and mix together. Brush over the lamb cutlets.

2. Preheat a ridged grill pan over high heat. Add the cutlets to the hot pan and cook for 4–5 minutes on each side.

3. Transfer to warm serving plates. Garnish with orange wedges and serve immediately.

1

1

2

GOES WELL WITH

For a stylish dinner party, serve with boiled new potatoes and a green salad.

Honeyed Apricot Lamb with Lemon Couscous

 SERVES 4   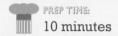 PREP TIME: 10 minutes   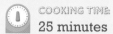 COOKING TIME: 25 minutes

nutritional information per serving	408 kcals, 10g fat, 3g sat fat, 23g total sugars, 0.6g salt

The combination of the honey, apricots, and spices offers a taste of Morocco to this speedy lamb stew, served with couscous.

INGREDIENTS

4 large lamb cutlets

4 teaspoons ground coriander

1 tablespoon ground cumin

1 small butternut squash

1 tablespoon olive oil

1 onion, chopped

2½ cups chicken stock

2 tablespoons chopped fresh ginger

⅔ cup dried apricots

2 tablespoons honey

finely grated rind and juice of 1 lemon

1 cup couscous

salt and pepper

3 tablespoons chopped fresh mint, to garnish

1. Sprinkle the lamb with the ground coriander and cumin. Peel and seed the squash and cut into bite-size chunks.

2. Heat the oil in a large flameproof casserole dish over medium heat. Add the lamb and cook over high heat for 2–3 minutes, turning once. Stir in the squash, onion, and half the stock, then bring to a boil.

3. Add the ginger, apricots, honey, and lemon juice and season with salt and pepper. Cover and cook over medium heat for about 20 minutes, stirring occasionally.

4. Meanwhile, bring the remaining stock to a boil in a small saucepan, then stir in the couscous and lemon rind and season with salt and pepper. Remove from the heat, cover, and let stand for 5 minutes.

5. Transfer the lamb to warm serving plates. Garnish with fresh mint and serve immediately with couscous.

Herbed Lamb Burgers

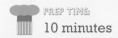 SERVES 4

 PREP TIME:
10 minutes

COOKING TIME:
6–8 minutes

nutritional information
per serving

521 cal, 18g fat, 7g sat fat, 5g total sugars, 1.9g salt

Ground lamb makes these excellent juicy burgers, packed full of fresh herbs, a great choice for a dinner.

INGREDIENTS

1 pound fresh lean ground lamb

1⅔ cups fresh bread crumbs

1 onion, finely chopped

3 tablespoons chopped fresh herbs, such as mint, rosemary, or thyme

1 egg

½ tablespoon apple juice

2 tablespoons vegetable oil

salt and pepper

to serve
lettuce leaves
4 hamburger buns
tomato slices

1. Put the lamb in a large mixing bowl. Add the bread crumbs, onion, chopped herbs, egg, and apple juice. Season with salt and pepper and mix together.

2. Divide the mixture into four portions, shape each into a ball, then flatten slightly to make a patty shape of your preferred thickness.

3. Heat the oil in a large skillet. Cook the burgers for 3–4 minutes on each side, until cooked all the way through.

4. Place the lettuce of the bottom halves on the buns and top with the tomato slices. Put the burgers on top and add the lids. Transfer to serving plates and serve immediately.

1

2

3

GOES WELL
WITH

Mix plain yogurt,
shredded cucumber,
(squeezed in a dish
towel to extract
excess water),
crushed garlic, and
chopped mint to
make an Indian
raita to serve with
the burger.

Pork in Plum Sauce

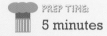 SERVES 4

 PREP TIME:
5 minutes

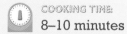 COOKING TIME:
8–10 minutes

nutritional information per serving	628 cal, 18g fat, 5g sat fat, 70g total sugars, 2.1g salt

Pork and plums go well together, and when combined in this super-speedy stir-fry with mushrooms, bean sprouts, and noodles, you'll forget about calling for a takeout.

INGREDIENTS

1¼ pounds pork tenderloin

2 tablespoons peanut oil

1 orange bell pepper, seeded and sliced

1 bunch scallions, sliced

8 ounces oyster mushrooms, sliced

3 cups fresh bean sprouts

2 tablespoons dry sherry

⅔ cup plum sauce

8 ounces medium egg noodles

salt and pepper

chopped fresh cilantro, to garnish

1. Slice the pork into long, thin strips. Preheat a wok or large skillet over high heat. Add the oil and heat until hot. Add the pork and stir-fry for 2–3 minutes. Add the orange bell pepper and stir-fry for 2 minutes, then add the scallions, mushrooms, and bean sprouts.

2. Stir-fry for 2–3 minutes, then add the sherry and plum sauce and heat until boiling. Season well with salt and pepper.

3. Meanwhile, cook the noodles in a saucepan of lightly salted boiling water according to the package directions, until tender. Drain well. Add to the wok.

4. Transfer to warm serving bowls. Garnish with chopped cilantro and serve immediately.

1

1

3

SOMETHING DIFFERENT Add a splash of extra color with some blanched green beans or broccoli.

Pork Pad Thai

 SERVES 4   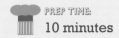 PREP TIME: 10 minutes   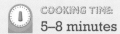 COOKING TIME: 5–8 minutes

nutritional information per serving	477 cal, 18g fat, 3.5g sat fat, 2.5g total sugars, 2g salt

Unless you make a trip to Thailand, where this dish is famous for being cooked in Bangkok's street markets, you can't get anything fresher or more delicious.

INGREDIENTS

8 ounces thick dried rice noodles

2 tablespoons peanut oil or vegetable oil

4 scallions, coarsely chopped

2 garlic cloves, crushed

2 red chiles, seeded and sliced

8 ounces pork tenderloin, trimmed and thinly sliced

4 ounces cooked, peeled large shrimp

juice of 1 lime

2 tablespoons Thai fish sauce

2 eggs, beaten

½ cup fresh bean sprouts

handful of chopped fresh cilantro

⅓ cup chopped unsalted peanuts

lime wedges, to serve

1. Prepare the noodles in a large saucepan of boiling water, covered, according to the package directions. Drain, rinse under cold running water, and set aside.

2. Preheat a wok or large skillet over high heat. Add the oil and heat until hot. Add the scallions, garlic, and chiles and stir-fry over medium–high heat for 1–2 minutes. Add the pork and stir-fry over high heat for 1–2 minutes, until browned all over.

3. Add the shrimp, lime juice, fish sauce, and eggs and stir-fry over medium heat for 2–3 minutes, until the eggs have set and the shrimp are heated through.

4. Add the bean sprouts, most of the cilantro, the peanuts, and the noodles and stir-fry for 30 seconds, until heated through.

5. Transfer to warm serving bowls. Garnish with the remaining cilantro and serve immediately with lime wedges.

2

3

4

Spicy Pork Meatballs

 SERVES 4   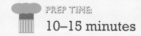 PREP TIME: 10–15 minutes   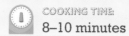 COOKING TIME: 8–10 minutes

nutritional information per serving	464 cal, 31g fat, 8g sat fat, 0.5g total sugars, trace salt

Make a batch of meatballs and freeze them. You can then defrost what you need for this recipe, or heat them in your favorite tomato sauce and serve with pasta.

INGREDIENTS

1½ pounds fresh lean ground pork

1 garlic clove, finely chopped

1 teaspoon ground ginger

pinch of ground cloves

½ teaspoon freshly grated nutmeg

½ teaspoon ground allspice

2 egg yolks

½ cup almond meal (ground almonds)

oil, for pan-frying

salt and pepper

mixed salad greens and crusty bread, to serve

1. Put the pork in a large mixing bowl. Add the garlic, spices, egg yolks, and almond meal. Season with salt and pepper and mix together. Use a small ice-cream scoop to shape the mixture into small balls.

2. Heat a shallow depth of oil in a deep skillet until hot. Add the meatballs in batches and sauté for 8–10 minutes, until cooked all the way through.

3. Lift out the meatballs with a slotted spoon and drain on absorbent paper towels.

4. Transfer to warm serving plates and serve immediately with salad greens and crusty bread.

1

1

2

Pepperoni Pasta

 SERVES 4    PREP TIME: 5 minutes   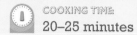 COOKING TIME: 20–25 minutes

nutritional information per serving	697 cal, 24g fat, 7g sat fat, 15g total sugars, 1g salt

This is a quick recipe, combining the flavors of a favorite pizza with a pasta sauce. A glass of Italian wine adds a wonderful finishing touch!

INGREDIENTS

3 tablespoons olive oil

1 onion, chopped

1 red bell pepper, seeded and diced

1 orange bell pepper, seeded and diced

1 (28-ounce) can diced tomatoes in juice

1 tablespoon sun-dried tomato paste

1 teaspoon paprika

8 ounces pepperoni sausage, sliced

2 tablespoons chopped fresh flat-leaf parsley, plus extra to garnish

1 pound dried penne

salt and pepper

crusty bread, to serve

1. Heat 2 tablespoons of the oil in a large, heavy skillet over medium heat. Add the onion and cook, stirring occasionally, for 5 minutes, or until softened.

2. Stir in the red bell pepper, orange bell pepper, tomatoes with their juices, sun-dried tomato paste, and paprika and bring to a boil.

3. Add the pepperoni and parsley and season with salt and pepper. Stir well and bring to a boil, then reduce the heat and simmer for 10–15 minutes.

4. Meanwhile, bring a large saucepan of lightly salted water to a boil. Add the pasta, bring back to a boil, and cook according to the package directions, until tender but still firm to the bite. Drain. Stir in the remaining oil, and toss to coat. Add the sauce and toss again.

5. Transfer to warm serving plates. Garnish with parsley and serve immediately with crusty bread.

Creamy Bolognese Pasta

 SERVES 4

 **PREP TIME:** 5 minutes

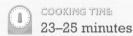 **COOKING TIME:** 23–25 minutes

nutritional information per serving	810 cal, 33g fat, 14g sat fat, 4g total sugars, 0.3g salt

This is a rich variation on a classic Italian Bolognese sauce, using pork instead of beef, and enriched with cream.

INGREDIENTS

2 tablespoons olive oil

1 onion, finely chopped

1 pound fresh ground pork

½ cup dry white wine

1 celery stalk, chopped

1 garlic clove, crushed

2 bay leaves

1 cup tomato puree

½ cup heavy cream

1 pound dried penne

1. Heat the oil in a large saucepan over high heat, add the onion and ground pork, and sauté, stirring, until lightly browned.

2. Stir in the wine, celery, garlic, bay leaves, and tomato puree and bring to a boil. Reduce the heat, cover, and simmer for 15 minutes.

3. Remove and discard the bay leaves. Stir in the cream and heat until boiling.

4. Meanwhile, bring a large saucepan of lightly salted water to a boil. Add the pasta, bring back to a boil, and cook according to the package directions, until tender but still firm to the bite. Drain and combine with the sauce.

5. Transfer to warm serving bowls and serve immediately.

FREEZING TIP
Freeze for up to
1 month. Or omit
the garlic and
freeze for up to
3 months. Defrost
in the refrigerator
or microwave before
reheating thoroughly.

Spaghetti with Bacon & Crispy Bread Crumbs

 SERVES 2

 PREP TIME: 10 minutes

 COOKING TIME: 8–10 minutes

nutritional information per serving	787 cal, 42g fat, 11g sat fat, 4g total sugars, 2.7g salt

Often the simplest dishes are the best, and when you're short on time, this one will come to the rescue.

INGREDIENTS

1 day-old ciabatta roll or 2 thick day-old ciabatta bread slices

6 ounces dried spaghetti

2 teaspoon olive oil

5 ounces smoked bacon, chopped

sprig of fresh rosemary, crushed

1 tablespoon butter

⅓ cup pine nuts

2 garlic cloves, crushed

2–3 tablespoons chopped fresh flat-leaf parsley

salt and pepper

1. Put the bread, including the crust, in a food processor or blender and process until the mixture resembles coarse bread crumbs.

2. Bring a large saucepan of lightly salted water to a boil. Add the pasta, bring back to a boil, and cook according to the package directions, until tender but still firm to the bite. Drain.

3. Meanwhile, heat the oil in a large skillet, add the bacon and rosemary and sauté for 2–3 minutes, until the bacon is golden brown. Remove from the skillet with a slotted spoon and set aside.

4. Add the butter to the bacon fat remaining in the skillet. When melted, add the bread crumbs, pine nuts, and garlic. Cook for 2–3 minutes, stirring until golden brown. Combine the bread-crumb mixture with the pasta along with the bacon and rosemary. Add the parsley and season with pepper.

5. Transfer to warm serving bowls and serve immediately.

3

3

4

Chorizo & Chickpea Casserole

 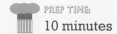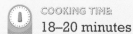

nutritional information per serving	500 cal, 21g fat, 6g sat fat, 8g total sugars, 1.3g salt

This recipe includes chorizo, a spicy Spanish sausage flavored with vibrant red smoked paprika.

INGREDIENTS

2 tablespoons olive oil

1 onion, sliced

1 large yellow bell pepper, seeded and sliced

1 garlic clove, crushed

1 teaspoon crushed red pepper

8 ounces chorizo sausage

1 (14½-ounce) can diced tomatoes

1 (15-ounce) can chickpeas, rinsed and drained

1 cup long-grain rice

handful of arugula

salt and pepper

¼ cup coarsely chopped fresh basil, to garnish

1. Heat the oil in a large flameproof casserole dish over medium heat. Add the onion and cook for 5 minutes, stirring occasionally.

2. Add the yellow bell pepper, garlic, and crushed red pepper, and cook for 2 minutes, stirring. Chop the chorizo into bite-size chunks and stir into the casserole.

3. Add the tomatoes and chickpeas and season with salt and pepper. Bring to a boil, cover, and simmer for 10 minutes.

4. Meanwhile, cook the rice in a saucepan of lightly salted boiling water for 10–12 minutes, until tender. Drain.

5. Stir the arugula into the casserole. Transfer to warm serving bowls. Garnish with fresh basil and serve immediately with the rice.

2

3

5

FREEZING TIP Omit the arugula and freeze for up to 1 month. Defrost and reheat, adding a little water, and stir in the arugula just before serving.

Pork & Rosemary Burgers

Pork makes great burgers and is a good choice for barbecues.

INGREDIENTS

1 pound fresh ground pork

1 small onion, finely chopped

1 garlic clove, crushed

1 tablespoon finely chopped fresh rosemary

oil, for brushing

¼ cup Greek-style yogurt

2 tablespoons chopped fresh mint

1 French baguette, split and cut into four

salt and pepper

tomato slices and pickle slices, to serve

1. Put the pork in a large mixing bowl. Add the onion, garlic, and rosemary. Season with salt and pepper and mix together.

2. Divide the mixture into four portions, shape each into a ball, then flatten slightly to make a patty shape of your preferred thickness.

3. Brush a ridged grill pan or skillet with oil. Cook the burgers for 3–4 minutes on each side, until cooked all the way through.

4. Meanwhile, place the yogurt and mint in a small bowl and mix together.

5. Place the burgers on the bottom halves of the baguette and top with the tomato slices and pickles. Add a spoonful of the minty yogurt and add the baguette tops. Transfer to serving plates and serve immediately.

2

3

5

SOMETHING DIFFERENT
Serve with a spicy
apple chutney,
salad, and potato
chips for an easy
weekend lunch.

Prosciutto & Red Pepper Pizza

 MAKES
1 PIZZA

 PREP TIME:
10 minutes

 COOKING TIME:
10 minutes

nutritional information per pizza	1,772 cal, 92g fat, 20g sat fat, 20g total sugars, 6g salt

Creating your own pizza is cheaper than buying prepared ones, and you can vary the toppings.

INGREDIENTS

2 tablespoons olive oil

1 (12-inch) store-bought pizza crust

¼ cup prepared red pesto sauce

1 small red bell pepper, seeded and thinly sliced

4 thin slices prosciutto

6 cherry tomatoes, halved

4 ounces mozzarella cheese, torn into pieces

1 teaspoon dried oregano

salt and pepper

1. Preheat the oven to 425°F. Brush a large baking sheet with a little oil and place the pizza crust on the sheet.

2. Spread the pesto sauce over the pizza crust to within ½-inch of the edge. Arrange the red bell pepper slices, prosciutto, and tomatoes over the pizza.

3. Sprinkle the mozzarella and oregano over the pizza, season with salt and pepper, then drizzle with the remaining olive oil.

4. Bake the pizza in the preheated oven for about 10 minutes, until bubbling and golden. Serve immediately.

SOMETHING DIFFERENT

For a vegetarian version, omit the prosciutto and replace with 3 artichoke hearts in oil (from a jar), drained and cut into halves or quarters.

Chicken Nuggets with Barbecue Sauce *118*

Oven-Fried Chicken Wings *120*

Yaki Soba *122*

Chicken-Fried Rice *124*

Garlic Chicken with Leeks *126*

Chicken with Creamy Penne *128*

Fettuccine with Chicken & Basil Pesto *130*

Cajun Chicken Gumbo *132*

Chicken Quesadillas *134*

Jerk Chicken Skewers with Rice *136*

Chicken & Herb Fritters *138*

Baked Tapenade Chicken *140*

Chicken Breasts with a Parmesan Crumb Topping *142*

Chicken with Prosciutto & Mozzarella *144*

Chicken Pot Pie *146*

Honey & Mustard Chicken *148*

Piri Piri Chicken *150*

Barbecued Chicken *152*

Ground Turkey Chili *154*

Turkey Schnitzel with Potato Wedges *156*

Ground Turkey Pasta *158*

Turkey Burger *160*

Turkey Cutlets with Prosciutto & Sage *162*

Stir-Fried Turkey with Cranberry Glaze *164*

Poultry

Chicken Nuggets
with Barbecue Sauce

 SERVES 4 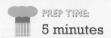 PREP TIME: 5 minutes  COOKING TIME: 10 minutes

nutritional information per serving	760 cal, 38g fat, 24g sat fat, 66g total sugars, 3g salt

Once you've tried this recipe, you won't want to bother with ordering the take-out version again.

INGREDIENTS

¼ cup dry bread crumbs

2 tablespoons grated Parmesan cheese

2 teaspoon chopped fresh thyme, or 1 teaspoon dried

2 skinless, boneless chicken breasts, cut into cubes

1 stick butter, melted

salt and pepper

barbecue sauce
4 tablespoons butter

2 large onions, grated

1¼ cups cider vinegar or wine vinegar

1¼ cups ketchup

¾ cup firmly packed dark brown sugar

1–2 teaspoon Worcestershire sauce

salt and pepper

1. Preheat the oven to 400°F. Put the bread crumbs, cheese, and thyme in a wide, shallow bowl. Season with salt and pepper and mix together.

2. Coat the chicken pieces in the melted butter, let any excess drip back into the dish, then coat in the crumb mixture.

3. Arrange the chicken pieces in a single layer on a large baking sheet. Bake in the preheated oven for 10 minutes, until the chicken is cooked all the way through.

4. Meanwhile, to make the sauce, heat the butter in a large saucepan over low heat. Add the onions and cook until soft but not brown. Add the vinegar, ketchup, sugar, and Worcestershire sauce. Season with salt and pepper and heat, stirring, until the sugar has dissolved completely. Bring to a boil, then reduce the heat and simmer for 5 minutes.

5. Transfer the chicken to a warm serving dish and serve immediately with the sauce.

Oven-Fried Chicken Wings

 SERVES 4    PREP TIME: 5 minutes    COOKING TIME: 20 minutes

nutritional information per serving	551 cal, 25g fat, 11g sat fat, 2g total sugars, 1.5g salt

These wings are wonderful served cold on a picnic. Bring along a blue cheese dressing with crispy carrot and celery sticks to accompany them.

INGREDIENTS

12 chicken wings
1 egg
¼ cup milk
⅓ cup all-purpose flour
1 teaspoon paprika
4 cups fresh bread crumbs
4 tablespoons butter, melted
salt and pepper

1. Preheat the oven to 425°F. Cut each of the chicken wings into three pieces. Discard the bony tip. Beat the egg with the milk in a wide, shallow dish. Put the flour and paprika in a separate wide, shallow dish, season with salt and pepper, and combine. Put the bread crumbs in another wide, shallow dish.

2. Dip the chicken pieces into the seasoned flour and coat first in the egg mixture, letting any excess drip back into the dish, then in the bread crumbs.

3. Pour the melted butter into a large, shallow roasting pan. Arrange the chicken pieces in a single layer in the pan. Bake in the preheated oven for 20 minutes, turning occasionally, until the chicken is tender and the juices run clear when the tip of a knife is inserted into the thickest part of the meat.

4. Transfer to a warm serving dish and serve immediately.

1

2

3

Yaki Soba

 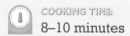
nutritional information per serving	584 cal, 13g fat, 2g sat fat, 10g total sugars, 3.7g salt

This recipe comes from Japan, although it probably originated in China as the well-known dish by the name of Chow Mein.

INGREDIENTS

1 pound ramen noodles

1 onion, finely sliced

2 cups bean sprouts

1 red bell pepper, seeded and sliced

1 cup cooked, sliced chicken

12 cooked, peeled shrimp

1 tablespoon oil, for stir-frying

2 tablespoons Japanese soy sauce or Chinese light soy sauce

1 teaspoon sesame oil

sesame seeds and finely sliced scallions, to garnish

1. Cook the noodles in a saucepan of lightly salted boiling water according to the package directions, until tender. Drain well and set aside.

2. Put the onion, bean sprouts, red pepper, chicken, and shrimp into a large mixing bowl. Add the noodles and mix together. Meanwhile, preheat a wok or large skillet over high heat. Add the oil and heat until hot.

3. Add the noodle mixture and stir-fry for 4 minutes. Add the soy sauce and sesame oil and toss together.

4. Transfer to warm serving bowls. Garnish with sesame seeds and scallions and serve immediately.

2

3

4

Chicken-Fried Rice

 SERVES 4    PREP TIME: 5 minutes   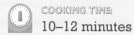 COOKING TIME: 10–12 minutes

nutritional information
per serving   423 cal, 10g fat, 2.5g sat fat, 12g total sugars, 2.5g salt

The quickest of dishes, this is ready in minutes and you can adapt the ingredients to suit yourself.

INGREDIENTS

½ cup long-grain rice
½ tablespoons sesame oil
6 shallots, peeled and cut into quarters
3 cups cubed, cooked chicken
3 tablespoons soy sauce
2 carrots, diced
1 celery stick, diced
1 red bell pepper, seeded and diced
1¼ cups fresh peas
⅔ cup canned corn, drained
2 extra-large eggs

1. Cook the rice in a saucepan of lightly salted water for 10–12 minutes, until tender. Drain.

2. Meanwhile, preheat a wok or large skillet over high heat. Add the oil and heat until hot.

3. Add the shallots and sauté until soft, then add the chicken and 2 tablespoons of the soy sauce and stir-fry for 5–6 minutes.

4. Stir in the carrots, celery, red pepper, peas, and corn and stir-fry for an additional 5 minutes.

5. Add the rice and stir thoroughly. Finally, beat the eggs and pour into the mixture. Stir until the eggs are beginning to set, then add in the remaining soy sauce.

6. Transfer to warm serving bowls and serve immediately.

COOK'S NOTE
Using cooked
chicken makes this
dish incredibly
quick to cook, so
it is perfect for
a quick supper.

Garlic Chicken with Leeks

 SERVES 4 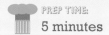 PREP TIME: 5 minutes 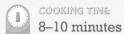 COOKING TIME: 8–10 minutes

nutritional information **per serving** | 200 cal, 5g fat, 1g sat fat, 9g total sugars, 1.5g salt

Chicken and leeks always taste great together and combine well with the unmistakable flavor of fresh ginger and soy sauce.

INGREDIENTS

1 pound skinless, boneless chicken breasts, finely chopped
1 tablespoon peanut oil
6 garlic cloves, thinly sliced
1-inch piece finely grated fresh ginger
2 leeks, thinly sliced
4 scallions, chopped
1 tablespoon honey

marinade
2 tablespoons rice wine
2 tablespoons dark soy sauce
1 teaspoon sesame oil

1. To make the marinade, pour the rice wine, soy sauce, and sesame oil into a large mixing bowl. Add the chicken strips and mix together.

2. Drain the chicken, reserving the marinade. Preheat a wok or large skillet over high heat. Add the oil and heat until hot. Add the drained chicken and stir-fry for 3 minutes to seal all around.

3. Add the garlic, ginger, leeks, and scallions to the wok and sauté for an additional 3 minutes to soften. Add the reserved marinade and honey and stir-fry for an additional minute, until the chicken is cooked all the way through.

4. Transfer to warm serving bowls and serve immediately.

1

2

3

GOES WELL WITH
Choose cooked rice,
or try noodles that
just need to be
softened in a bowl
of boiling water.

Chicken with Creamy Penne

 SERVES 2   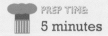 PREP TIME: 5 minutes   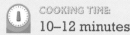 COOKING TIME: 10–12 minutes

nutritional information per serving	810 cal, 30g fat, 14g sat fat, 4g total sugars, 0.3g salt

The white wine and cream turn a simple chicken-and-pasta dish into something special.

INGREDIENTS

8 ounces dried penne

1 tablespoon olive oil

2 skinless, boneless chicken breasts

¼ cup dry white wine

¾ cup frozen peas

⅓ cup heavy cream

¼–⅓ cup chopped fresh parsley, to garnish

salt

1. Bring a large saucepan of lightly salted water to a boil. Add the pasta, bring back to a boil, and cook according to the package directions, until tender but still firm to the bite.

2. Meanwhile, heat the oil in a skillet over medium heat. Add the chicken breasts and cook, turning once, for 8–10 minutes, until the chicken is tender and the juices run clear when the tip of a knife is inserted into the thickest part of the meat.

3. Pour in the wine and cook over high heat until it has almost evaporated.

4. Drain the pasta. Add the peas, cream, and pasta to the skillet and stir well. Cover and simmer for 2 minutes.

5. Transfer to warm serving plates. Garnish with fresh parsley and serve immediately.

HEALTHY HINT Instead of heavy cream, add low-fat Greek-style yogurt.

Fettuccine with Chicken & Basil Pesto

 SERVES 4

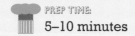 PREP TIME: 5–10 minutes

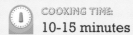 COOKING TIME: 10-15 minutes

nutritional information per serving	895 cal, 46g fat, 9g sat fat, 2.5g total sugars, 0.7g salt

No time to make pesto? Then use one of the many excellent brands in your supermarket.

INGREDIENTS

2 tablespoons vegetable oil

4 skinless, boneless chicken breasts

12 ounces dried fettuccine

salt and pepper

sprig of fresh basil, to garnish

pesto

2½ cups shredded fresh basil

½ cup extra-virgin olive oil

3 tablespoons pine nuts

3 garlic cloves, crushed

⅔ cup freshly grated Parmesan cheese

2 tablespoons freshly grated Pecorino cheese

salt

1. To make the pesto, put the basil, olive oil, pine nuts, garlic, and a generous pinch of salt in a food processor or blender and process until smooth. Transfer the mixture to a bowl and stir in the cheeses.

2. Heat the oil in a large skillet over medium heat. Add the chicken breasts and cook for 8–10 minutes, turning once, until the chicken is tender and the juices run clear when the tip of a knife is inserted into the thickest part of the meat. Cut into small cubes.

3. Meanwhile, bring a large saucepan of lightly salted water to a boil. Add the pasta, bring back to a boil, and cook according to the package directions, until tender but still firm to the bite. Drain and transfer to a warm serving dish. Add the chicken and pesto, then season with salt and pepper and mix together.

4. Transfer to warm serving plates. Garnish with sprigs of basil and serve immediately.

Cajun Chicken Gumbo

 SERVES 2  PREP TIME: 5 minutes  COOKING TIME: 20 minutes

nutritional information
per serving   463 cal, 9g fat, 1.5g sat fat, 8g total sugars, 0.8g salt

This is a spicy chicken stew from the Deep South. It's a great dish to make when you have to feed a crowd.

INGREDIENTS

1 tablespoon sunflower oil

4 chicken thighs

1 small onion, diced

2 celery stalks, diced

1 small green bell pepper, seeded and diced

½ cup long-grain rice

1¼ cup chicken stock

1 fresh red chile, thinly sliced

20 okra pods, trimmed, (about 9 ounces)

1 tablespoon tomato paste

salt and pepper

1. Heat the oil in a large skillet over medium heat. Add the chicken and cook until golden. Remove the chicken from the skillet using a slotted spoon. Add the onion, celery, and green bell pepper to the skillet and cook for 1 minute. Pour off any excess fat.

2. Add the rice and cook, stirring briskly, for an additional minute. Add the chicken stock and bring to a boil.

3. Add the chile and okra to the skillet with the tomato paste. Season with salt and pepper.

4. Return the chicken to the skillet and stir. Cover tightly and simmer gently for for 15 minutes, until all the liquid has been absorbed, the chicken is tender, and the juices run clear when the tip of a sharp knife is inserted into the thickest part of the meat. Stir occasionally, and add a little extra stock is the mixture becomes too dry. Transfer to warm serving plates and serve immediately.

1

1

3

Chicken Quesadillas

 SERVES 4    PREP TIME: 15 minutes    COOKING TIME: 30 minutes

nutritional information per serving	767 cal, 31g fat, 14g sat fat, 5g total sugars, 2.3g salt

These make a wonderful snack and a great choice for when friends come over. Try them with other fillings, too.

INGREDIENTS

3–4 tablespoons sunflower oil

1 red onion, thinly sliced

1 pound skinless, boneless chicken breasts, finely chopped

1 yellow bell pepper, seeded and thinly sliced

1 teaspoon chili powder

8 flour tortillas

½ cup mild salsa

1¾ cups shredded cheddar cheese,

¼ cup chopped fresh cilantro

salt and pepper

to serve

sour cream

guacamole

lime wedges

1. Heat 1 tablespoon of the oil in a skillet and sauté the onion for 5 minutes, until softened. Add the chicken and yellow bell pepper and cook over medium–high heat, stirring frequently, for 10–12 minutes, until the chicken is cooked all the way through. Stir in the chili powder and season with salt and pepper.

2. Take one of the tortillas and spread with 2 tablespoons of the salsa, leaving a ½-inch border around the edge of the tortilla. Spread one-quarter of the chicken mixture over the salsa, then sprinkle one-quarter of the shredded cheese and cilantro over the chicken mixture. Place a second tortilla on top, pressing down gently. Repeat with the remaining ingredients to make four quesadillas in total.

3. Heat a little of the remaining oil in a large skillet and cook the quesadillas, one at a time, for 3–4 minutes on each side, until crisp and lightly browned, adding more oil when necessary.

4. Transfer to warm serving plates. Serve immediately with sour cream, guacamole, and lime wedges.

Jerk Chicken Skewers with Rice

 SERVES 4

 PREP TIME: 10 minutes

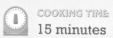 COOKING TIME: 15 minutes

nutritional information per serving	372 cal, 9g fat, 2g sat fat, 1g total sugars, 0.3g salt

These chicken skewers have a moist, spicy coating to keep them juicy and full of flavor.

INGREDIENTS

1 pound chicken thighs, cut into bite-size chunks
1 cup long-grain rice
1 tablespoon grated lime rind
2 tablespoons cilantro
salt
lime wedges, to serve

jerk sauce
1 small onion, quartered
1 garlic clove
2 green finger chiles
1-inch piece fresh ginger
1 teaspoon ground allspice
1½ teaspoon dried thyme
juice of ½ lime
2 tablespoons olive oil

1. Soak eight wooden skewers in water for 30 minutes to prevent them from charring. Meanwhile, preheat the broiler to high. Make the sauce by putting all the ingredients in a food processor or blender and processing until smooth. Transfer to a bowl and stir in the chunks of chicken. Cover and let stand for 5 minutes.

2. Cook the rice in a saucepan of lightly salted water according to the package directions, until tender. Drain. Stir in the lime rind and cilantro, cover the pan with a clean dish towel, and let stand.

3. Thread the chicken onto the eight presoaked, wooden skewers. Cook the skewers under the preheated broiler for 12–15 minutes, turning occasionally, until the chicken is cooked all the way through.

4. Transfer to warm serving plates. Serve immediately with the lime and cilantro rice and lime wedges.

1

1

2

COOK'S NOTE
The jerk sauce is hot and spicy, but if you prefer a milder flavor, halve the chiles and remove the seeds before using.

Chicken & Herb Fritters

 SERVES 4  PREP TIME: 5 minutes 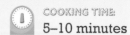 COOKING TIME: 5–10 minutes

nutritional information
per serving

468 cal, 18g fat, 6g sat fat, 2g total sugars, 2g salt

Although these fritters are perfect when you have leftovers, they are so delicious that you might decide to make them from scratch.

INGREDIENTS

2⅓ cups mashed potatoes, with butter

1¾ cups chopped, cooked chicken

1 cup finely chopped, cooked ham

1 tablespoon fresh mixed herbs

2 eggs, lightly beaten

1 tablespoon milk

2¾ cups fresh wheat bread crumbs

oil, for pan-frying

salt and pepper

mixed salad greens, to serve

1. Put the potatoes, chicken, ham, herbs, and one of the eggs in a large mixing bowl. Season with salt and pepper and mix together.

2. Divide the mixture into small portions and shape each into a ball.

3. Beat the remaining egg with the milk in a wide, shallow dish. Place the bread crumbs in a separate wide, shallow dish.

4. Coat the chicken balls in the egg mixture, letting any excess drip back into the dish, then in the bread crumbs.

5. Heat the oil in a large skillet over medium heat and cook the fritters until they are golden brown.

6. Transfer to a warm serving dish and serve immediately with mixed salad greens.

1

2

3

Baked Tapenade Chicken

 SERVES 4   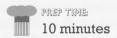 PREP TIME: 10 minutes    COOKING TIME: 25 minutes

nutritional information per serving | 574 cal, 25g fat, 6g sat fat, 4g total sugars, 2.6g salt

Tapenade is a thick paste made from black or green olives—sometimes sundried tomatoes, too.

INGREDIENTS

4 skinless, boneless chicken breasts

¼ cup green olive tapenade

8 thin slices smoked pancetta

2 garlic cloves, chopped

15 cherry tomatoes, halved

½ cup dry white wine

2 tablespoons olive oil

8 slices ciabatta

salt and pepper

1. Preheat the oven to 425°F. Cut three deep slits into each chicken breast. Spread a tablespoon of the tapenade over each chicken breast, pushing it into the slashes. Wrap each chicken breast in two slices of pancetta.

2. Place the chicken breasts in an ovenproof dish and arrange the garlic and tomatoes around them. Season with salt and pepper, pour the wine over the chicken, and sprinkle with 1 tablespoon of the oil.

3. Bake in the preheated oven for 20 minutes, until the chicken is tender and the juices run clear when the tip of a sharp knife or skewer is inserted into the thickest part of the meat. Cover the dish loosely with aluminum foil and let stand for 5 minutes.

4. Meanwhile, preheat the broiler to high. Brush the ciabatta with the remaining oil and cook under the preheated broiler for 2–3 minutes, turning once, until golden.

5. Transfer to serving plates. Serve immediately with the ciabatta.

1
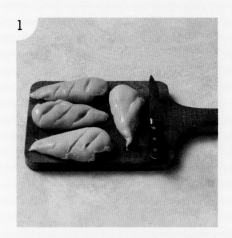

1

3

BE PREPARED
Prepare the recipe earlier in the day. Place in an oven-proof dish and cover tightly before refrigerating—the tapenade smell can transfer to other foods. Let reach room temperature, then cook as directed.

Chicken Breasts with a Parmesan Crumb Topping

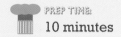 SERVES 4    PREP TIME: 10 minutes   COOKING TIME: 20 minutes

nutritional information per serving	355 cal, 18g fat, 2.5g sat fat, 0.5g total sugars, 0.7g salt

The combination of lemon and basil with a crunchy coating turns simple chicken breasts into a memorable main course.

INGREDIENTS

4 skinless, boneless chicken breasts
⅓ cup pesto sauce
1 cup ciabatta bread crumbs
¼ cup grated Parmesan cheese
finely grated rind of ½ lemon
2 tablespoons olive oil
salt and pepper
roasted vine tomatoes, to serve

1. Preheat the oven to 425°F. Cut a deep slit into each chicken breast to make a pocket. Open out the chicken breasts and spread 1 tablespoon of the pesto into each pocket. Fold the chicken flesh back over the pesto and place in an ovenproof dish.

2. Mix the remaining pesto with the bread crumbs, Parmesan cheese, and lemon rind. Spread the bread-crumb mixture over the chicken breasts. Season with salt and pepper and drizzle with the oil.

3. Bake in the preheated oven for 20 minutes, until the chicken is tender and the juices run clear when the tip of a knife is inserted into the thickest part of the meat.

4. Transfer to warm serving plates and serve immediately with roasted tomatoes.

1

1

2

Chicken with Prosciutto & Mozzarella

 SERVES 4   PREP TIME: 5 minutes   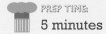 COOKING TIME: 20–25 minutes

nutritional information
per serving   300 cal, 10g fat, 6g sat fat, 2g total sugars, 1g salt

Chicken breasts are low in fat, but the mozzarella and ham keep them moist and tasty.

INGREDIENTS

4 skinless chicken breast fillets
5 ounces mozzarella cheese
8 large basil leaves
4 thin slices prosciutto
3 tablespoons dry white wine
1 cup tomato puree
salt and pepper
salad greens, to serve

1. Preheat the oven to 425°F. Cut a slit into each chicken breast to make a pocket. Divide the mozzarella into four pieces and wrap each in basil leaves. Open out the chicken breasts and tuck one mozzarella and basil leaf bundle into each pocket. Wrap each chicken breast in a slice of prosciutto.

2. Arrange the chicken breasts in a large, roasting pan. Pour the wine and tomato puree over the breasts and season with salt and pepper. Bake in the preheated oven for 20–25 minutes, turning occasionally, until the chicken is tender and the juices run clear when the tip of a knife is inserted into the thickest part of the meat.

3. Transfer to warm serving plates and serve immediately with salad greens.

BE PREPARED
If you're entertaining, the dish can be assembled earlier in the day, or the day before, then covered and chilled until you're ready to cook.

Chicken Pot Pie

 SERVES 4

 PREP TIME:
10 minutes

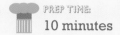 COOKING TIME:
25–30 minutes

nutritional information per serving	738 cal, 47g fat, 18g sat fat, 3g total sugars, 1.2g salt

Rolled dough pie crust is a great staple standby that saves on preparation time, and mess, when making pies.

INGREDIENTS

2 tablespoons olive oil

1 pound chicken breast, cut into strips

2 cups baby button mushrooms

1 bunch scallions, chopped

½ cup crème fraîche or heavy cream

¼ cup chicken stock

1 sheet of rolled dough pie crust

beaten egg or milk, to glaze

salt and pepper

green vegetables, to serve

1. Preheat the oven to 425°F. Place a baking sheet in the oven to preheat.

2. Heat the oil in a large skillet over high heat. Add the chicken and cook for 2–3 minutes, stirring frequently, until sealed all around. Add the mushrooms and onions and cook for an additional 2 minutes.

3. Add the crème fraîche and stock, season with salt and pepper, then transfer to a 1½-quart shallow ovenproof metal pie plate.

4. Lift the rolled dough on top, scrunching the edges in with your fingers to fit inside the rim of the pie plate. Make a small slit in the center and brush with beaten egg to glaze.

5. Place the pie plate on the preheated baking sheet and bake for 20–25 minutes, until the pastry is golden and firm. Transfer to warm serving plates and serve immediately with green vegetables.

SOMETHING
DIFFERENT
For a different
flavor, try
replacing the
chicken with
turkey breast
strips, and
replace the stock
with dry white
wine or vermouth.

Honey & Mustard Chicken

 SERVES 4

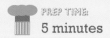 PREP TIME:
5 minutes

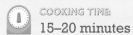 COOKING TIME:
15–20 minutes

nutritional information
per serving | 282 cal, 14g fat, 4g sat fat, 5g total sugars, 1.1g salt

Mildly sweet and spicy, these irresistible chicken pieces are a good choice for picnics or lunch boxes.

INGREDIENTS

8 chicken pieces
(drumsticks, thighs, wings)
2 tablespoons Dijon mustard
2 tablespoons
Worcestershire sauce
1 tablespoon honey
salt and pepper
crusty bread, to serve

1. Preheat the oven to 425°F. Trim any excess fat from the chicken and cut deep slashes into the thickest parts of the meat.

2. Put the mustard, Worcestershire sauce, and honey in a large mixing bowl. Season with salt and pepper and mix together. Add the chicken and turn to coat evenly.

3. Arrange the chicken in a single layer in a large, shallow roasting pan. Bake in the preheated oven for 15–20 minutes, turning occasionally, until the chicken is tender and the juices run clear when the tip of a knife is inserted into the thickest part of the meat.

4. Transfer to a warm serving dish and serve immediately with crusty bread.

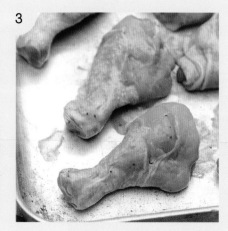

COOK'S NOTE
If there is time, let
the chicken marinate
in the mustard
coating for an hour
or so, or overnight,
chilled, to let the
flavors develop.

Piri Piri Chicken

SERVES 4

PREP TIME: 5 minutes

COOKING TIME: 20–25 minutes

nutritional information per serving	164 cal, 4g fat, 1.5g sat fat, 0g total sugars, 0.4g salt

This fiery chicken dish originates from Portugal, where the name refers to a particular type of hot chile.

INGREDIENTS

8 chicken drumsticks
1½ teaspoon crushed red pepper
2 garlic cloves, crushed
1 teaspoon dried oregano
2 teaspoon smoked paprika
juice of ½ lemon
salt and pepper

to serve
lemon wedges
mixed salad greens
flatbread

1. Preheat the oven to 425°F. Cut deep slashes into the thickest parts of the meat.

2. Put the crushed red pepper, garlic, oregano, paprika, and lemon juice in a large mixing bowl. Season with salt and pepper and mix together. Add the chicken and turn to coat evenly.

3. Arrange the chicken in a single layer in a large, shallow roasting pan. Bake in the preheated oven for 20–25 minutes, turning occasionally, until the chicken is tender and the juices run clear when the tip of a knife is inserted into the thickest part of the meat.

4. Transfer to warm serving plates. Serve immediately with lemon wedges, mixed salad greens, and flatbread.

1

2

2

HEALTHY HINT
If you're trying to cut down on fat, remove the chicken skin before coating in the sauce. Use paper towels to grip the skin and pull to remove.

Barbecued Chicken

 SERVES 4    PREP TIME: 5 minutes   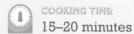 COOKING TIME: 15–20 minutes

nutritional information **per serving** | 211 cal, 7g fat, 1.5g sat fat, 5g total sugars, 2.1g salt

Who can resist a piece of sticky barbecued chicken, with its sweet and spicy, finger-licking glaze?

INGREDIENTS

8 skinless chicken thighs
⅓ cup ketchup
2 tablespoons soy sauce
1 tablespoon grated fresh ginger
1 garlic clove, crushed
1 tablespoon olive oil
salt and pepper
mixed salad greens and cooked rice, to serve

1. Preheat the oven to 425°F. Cut deep slashes into the thickest parts of the meat.

2. Put the ketchup, soy sauce, ginger, garlic, and oil in a large mixing bowl. Season with salt and pepper and mix together. Add the chicken and turn to coat evenly.

3. Arrange the chicken in a single layer in a large, shallow roasting pan. Bake in the preheated oven for 15–20 minutes, turning occasionally, until the chicken is tender and the juices run clear when the tip of a knife is inserted into the thickest part of the meat.

4. Transfer to warm serving plates and serve immediately with mixed salad greens and cooked rice.

1
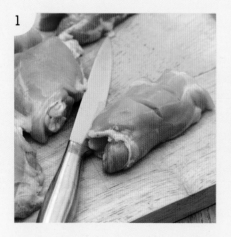

2

2

SOMETHING
DIFFERENT
Try cooking these
chicken pieces under
the broiler. Preheat the
broiler to high, then
broil for 15–20 minutes,
turning occasionally,
until cooked all
the way through.

Ground Turkey Chili

 SERVES 4

 PREP TIME:
10 minutes

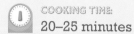 COOKING TIME:
20–25 minutes

nutritional information
per serving

270 cal, 7g fat, 1g sat fat, 5g total sugars, 1g salt

This simple one-dish meal, packed with spicy flavors, is great for a midweek family meal or informal party.

INGREDIENTS

2 tablespoons olive oil

1 large onion, diced

1 pound ground turkey

1 garlic clove, crushed

1 (14½-ounce) can diced tomatoes

1 (15-ounce) can cranberry beans, drained

1 cup chicken stock

2 teaspoon crushed red pepper

1 teaspoon dried thyme

salt and pepper

sour cream and tortilla chips, to serve

1. Heat the oil in a large saucepan over high heat, add the onion and ground turkey and sauté, stirring, until lightly browned.

2. Stir in the garlic, tomatoes, beans, stock, crushed red pepper, and thyme. Season with salt and pepper. Stir until boiling, then reduce the heat, cover, and simmer for 20 minutes, stirring occasionally.

3. Transfer to warm serving bowls and serve immediately with sour cream and tortilla chips.

GOES WELL
WITH
To complete the
meal, add a fresh
green salad of
shredded crisp
lettuce with chunks
of cooling cucumber
and avocado.

Turkey Schnitzel with Potato Wedges

 SERVES 4    PREP TIME: 15 minutes    COOKING TIME: 25 minutes

> nutritional information per serving : 518 cal, 17.5g fat, 4.5g sat fat, 1.5g total sugars, 0.7g salt

This method originated in Austria, where the traditional meat used is veal, but turkey also works well.

INGREDIENTS

4 potatoes

2 tablespoons olive oil, plus extra for pan-frying

1 tablespoon dried sage

1¼ cups fresh white bread crumbs

½ cup finely grated Parmesan cheese

4 thinly sliced turkey cutlets

1 egg, beaten

salt and pepper

lemon wedges, to serve

1. Preheat the oven to 425°F. Cut each potato into eight wedges. Put the potatoes, oil, and 1 teaspoon of sage into a large mixing bowl. Season with salt and pepper and turn to coat evenly. Arrange the potatoes in a single layer on a baking sheet. Bake in the preheated oven for 25 minutes, until golden brown and tender.

2. Meanwhile, put the bread crumbs, cheese, and remaining sage into a wide, shallow dish. Season with salt and pepper and mix together. Dip the turkey in the beaten egg and then in the crumb mixture, pressing to coat on both sides.

3. Heat a shallow depth of oil in a skillet over high heat, add the turkey, and cook for 4–5 minutes, turning once, until the turkey is tender and and cooked all the way through.

4. Transfer to warm serving plates and serve immediately with the potato wedges and lemon wedges.

1

2

2

GOES WELL
WITH
A fresh
tomato salad
makes a great
accompaniment,
with a drizzle
of olive oil and a
dash of balsamic
vinegar for a
simple dressing.

Ground Turkey Pasta

 SERVES 4   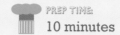 PREP TIME: 10 minutes    COOKING TIME: 25–30 minutes

nutritional information
per serving | 418 cal, 8g fat, 1.5g sat fat, 7.5g total sugars, 0.2g salt

Pasta is a useful staple for midweek meals, and this dish is sure to become a family favorite.

INGREDIENTS

2 tablespoons olive oil

1 red onion, diced

1 pound ground turkey

1 garlic clove, crushed

1 yellow bell pepper, seeded and diced

4 plum tomatoes, diced

⅔ cup red wine or chicken stock

1 tablespoon dried oregano

8 ounces dried penne

salt and pepper

¼–⅓ cup chopped fresh parsley, to garnish

1. Heat the oil in a large saucepan over high heat, add the onion and ground turkey, and sauté for 3–4 minutes, stirring, until lightly browned.

2. Stir in the garlic, yellow bell pepper, and tomatoes, then add the wine and oregano. Season with salt and pepper. Bring to a boil and boil rapidly for 2 minutes. Reduce the heat, cover, and simmer for 20 minutes, stirring occasionally.

3. Meanwhile, bring a large saucepan of lightly salted water to a boil. Add the pasta, bring back to a boil, and cook according to the package directions, until tender but still firm to the bite. Drain and combine with the sauce.

4. Transfer to warm serving bowls. Garnish with parsley and serve immediately.

1

2

2

SOMETHING DIFFERENT

Try turning this recipe into a vegetarian dish by replacing the turkey with meat-free soy protein crumble. If you're adding stock instead of wine, use vegetable stock.

Turkey Burger

SERVES 4

PREP TIME:
10 minutes

COOKING TIME:
10–12 minutes

nutritional information
per serving | 493 cal, 19g fat, 3.5g sat fat, 3g total sugars, 1.5g salt

Lean ground turkey is a good choice if you are cutting down on fat in your diet.

INGREDIENTS

1 pound ground turkey
1 small red onion, finely chopped
1 garlic clove, crushed
1 tablespoon finely chopped rosemary
1 tablespoon sunflower oil, for brushing
salt and pepper

to serve
1 Boston lettuce, shredded
4 sesame hamburger buns
2 small pickles, sliced
⅓ cup mayonnaise

1. Preheat the broiler to medium–high. Put the turkey in a large mixing bowl. Add the onion, garlic, and rosemary. Season with salt and pepper and mix together.

2. Divide the mixture into four portions, shape each into a ball, then flatten slightly to make a patty shape of your preferred thickness. Brush lightly with the oil.

3. Cook the burgers under the preheated broiler for about 5–6 minutes on each side, until cooked all the way through.

4. Place the lettuce on the bottom halves of the buns and top with the burgers. Put the pickles and a spoonful of mayonnaise on top and add the lids. Serve immediately.

1

2

2

TO SERVE
Freeze freshly made
burgers for up to
1 month, or 3 months,
if you omit the
garlic. Interleave
with wax paper,
and thaw completely
before cooking.

Turkey Cutlets with Prosciutto & Sage

 SERVES 2    PREP TIME: 10 minutes   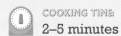 COOKING TIME: 2–5 minutes

nutritional information per serving	412 cal, 20g fat, 6.5g sat fat, 0.5g total sugars, 0.9g salt

This recipe is similar to a traditional Italian dish, known as Saltimbocca alla Romana, which is made with slices of veal.

INGREDIENTS

2 skinless, boneless turkey cutlets
2 slices proscuitto, halved
4 fresh sage leaves
2 tablespoons all-purpose flour
2 tablespoons olive oil
1 tablespoon butter
salt and pepper
lemon wedges, to serve

1. Slice the turkey cutlets in half horizontally into 2 thinner cutlets. Put the cutlets between 2 sheets of plastic wrap and pound lightly with a rolling pin. Season with salt and pepper. Lay half a slice of prosciutto on each cutlet, put a sage leaf on top, and secure with a toothpick.

2. Put the flour in a wide, shallow dish and season with salt and pepper. Dust each side of the cutlet with the seasoned flour.

3. Heat the oil in a large skillet, add the butter, and cook until foaming. Add the cutlets and cook over medium heat for 1½ minutes, sage-side down. Turn the cutlets over and cook for another 30 seconds, until the turkey is tender and cooked all the way through.

4. Transfer to warm serving plates and serve immediately with lemon wedges.

1

1

3

GOES WELL WITH Serve with new potatoes and a crisp salad of arugula and watercress.

Stir-Fried Turkey with Cranberry Glaze

PREP TIME: 5 minutes   COOKING TIME: 10–12 minutes

nutritional information per serving	250 cal, 7g fat, 1g sat fat, 11g total sugars, 2.2 g salt

Using canned chestnuts instead of fresh chestnuts makes this recipe incredibly quick and easy.

INGREDIENTS

2 tablespoons sunflower oil

1 pound turkey breasts, skinned and cut into strips

1 piece preserved ginger, drained and finely chopped

½ cup fresh or frozen cranberries

9 canned chestnuts

¼ cup cranberry sauce

3 tablespoons light soy sauce

salt and pepper

1. Preheat a wok or large skillet over high heat. Add the oil and heat until hot. Add the turkey to the wok and stir-fry for 5 minutes, until golden brown and cooked all the way through.

2. Add the ginger and the cranberries to the wok and stir-fry for 2–3 minutes, or until the cranberries have softened. Add the chestnuts, cranberry sauce, and soy sauce, season with salt and pepper, and let bubble for 2–3 minutes.

3. Transfer to warm serving bowls and serve immediately.

Sole Fish Cakes *168*

Fish Sticks with Chili Mayonnaise *170*

Sea Bass with Spicy Sauce *172*

Crispy Parmesan-Coated Sea Bass *174*

Sea Bass with Olive Gremolata *176*

Monkfish with a Lemon & Parsley Crust *178*

Rustic Fish Casserole *180*

Quick & Creamy Fish Gratin *182*

Grilled Salmon Steak with Noodles *184*

Salmon with Lentil Salad *186*

Smoked Salmon with Tagliatelle *188*

Farfalle with Salmon & Vegetables *190*

Spicy Tuna Fish Cakes *192*

Pasta with Tuna & Olives *194*

Grilled Tuna with Lemon, Capers & Thyme *196*

Tuna Noodle Casserole *198*

Quick Paella *200*

Spicy Thai Seafood Stew *202*

Seafood Risotto *204*

Mixed Seafood Pasta *206*

Calamari with Shrimp *208*

Thai Shrimp Noodle Bowl *210*

Spaghetti with Shrimp & Garlic *212*

Tagliatelle with Mussels in White Wine *214*

Fish & Seafood

Sole Fish Cakes

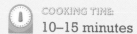
nutritional information
per serving | 304 cal, 15g fat, 4g sat fat, 2g total sugars, 0.3g salt

This is an excellent way to use up leftover mashed potatoes;
if you don't have leftovers, use store-bought mashed potatoes.

INGREDIENTS

1 pound skinless sole fillet
2 cups mashed potatoes
4 scallions, finely chopped
2 tablespoons chopped parsley
1 medium egg, beaten
all-purpose flour, for shaping
sunflower oil, for pan-frying
salt and pepper
green vegetables and lemon
wedges, to serve

1. Place the sole in a wide saucepan and add just enough boiling water to cover. Bring to a boil, then reduce the heat, cover, and simmer for 4–5 minutes, until the fish flakes easily. Drain thoroughly.

2. Place the fish in a large mixing bowl. Add the mashed potatoes, scallions, parsley, and egg. Season with salt and pepper and mix together.

3. Divide the mixture into eight portions and shape each into a ball. Then, on a floured surface, flatten slightly to make a patty shape of your preferred thickness.

4. Heat a shallow depth of oil in a large skillet until hot. Add the fish cakes in two batches and cook for 6–8 minutes, turning once, until golden brown. Drain on paper towels.

5. Transfer to warm serving plates and serve immediately with green vegetables and lemon wedges.

2

3

4

Fish Sticks with Chili Mayonnaise

 SERVES 4    PREP TIME: 5 minutes   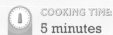 COOKING TIME: 5 minutes

nutritional information per serving	574 cal, 26g fat, 4g sat fat, 6g total sugars, 0.9g salt

Matzo meal, a traditional Jewish ingredient, is made by grinding the cracker-like matzo bread into crumbs.

INGREDIENTS

1⅔ cups all-purpose flour

3 eggs, beaten

1¼ cups matzo meal

1 pound firm white fish fillets, such as flounder, halibut, or red snapper, cut into strips

sunflower oil or peanut oil, for pan-frying

salt and pepper

chili mayonnaise

2 tablespoons sweet chili sauce

4–5 tablespoons mayonnaise

1. Put the flour in a wide, shallow dish. Season with salt and pepper and mix together. Put the beaten egg in a bowl. Put the matzo meal in a separate wide, shallow dish.

2. Dip the fish pieces into the seasoned flour, then coat in the egg mixture, letting any excess drip back into the dish, then in the matzo meal.

3. Heat the oil in a large skillet and cook the fish pieces in batches, until they are golden brown and cooked all the way through.

4. To make the chili mayonnaise, put the chili sauce and mayonnaise in a bowl and mix together.

5. Transfer the fish to warm serving plates and serve immediately with the chili mayonnaise.

1

3

4

Sea Bass with Spicy Sauce

 SERVES 4  PREP TIME: 5 minutes 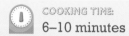 COOKING TIME: 6–10 minutes

nutritional information per serving | 397 cal, 13g fat, 2g sat fat, 30g total sugars, 1.9g salt

Sea bass is one of the easiest fish to cook and goes well with this rich, spicy tomato sauce.

INGREDIENTS

8 small sea bass fillets
2 tablespoons olive oil
salt and pepper
snipped chives, to garnish
mashed potatoes, to serve

sauce

1 tablespoon olive oil
2 garlic cloves, crushed
1 small red finger chile, seeded and finely chopped
1 (14½-ounce) can diced tomatoes
1 tablespoon soy sauce
2 teaspoon honey
salt and pepper

1. To make the sauce, put the oil into a large saucepan with the garlic and chile and heat until they begin to sizzle, then stir in the tomatoes and bring to a boil. Add the soy sauce and honey and season with salt and pepper. Simmer for 2–3 minutes to reduce slightly. Keep warm.

2. Brush the fish fillets with oil and season with salt and pepper. Heat a large, heavy skillet until hot, add the fish fillets, and cook for 2–3 minutes on each side, until firm.

3. Transfer to warm serving plates. Garnish with chives and serve immediately with the sauce and mashed potatoes.

1

1

2

Crispy Parmesan-Coated Sea Bass

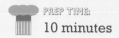 SERVES 4    PREP TIME: 10 minutes    COOKING TIME: 4 minutes

nutritional information per serving	303 cal, 19g fat, 6.5g sat fat, 0.2g total sugars, 0.7g salt

Simple yet elegant, this dish is all about the quality of the ingredients.

INGREDIENTS

3 tablespoons olive oil

4 sea bass fillets, about 4 ounces each, skin on and pin-boned

juice and grated rind of 1 lemon

1 cup finely grated Parmesan cheese

1 small bunch fresh parsley, finely chopped

salt and pepper

mixed salad greens and lemon wedges, to serve

1. Preheat the broiler to high. Line the broiler pan with aluminum foil or brush it with a little of the oil. Lay the fillets in the broiler pan, skin-side down. Drizzle the lemon juice over the fish along with a little of the remaining oil. Season with salt and pepper.

2. Put the lemon rind, Parmesan cheese, and parsley in a large mixing bowl and mix together. Sprinkle the mixture evenly over the fish and drizzle with the remaining oil.

3. Cook the fish under the preheated broiler for 4 minutes, until golden brown and cooked all the way through.

4. Transfer to warm serving plates and serve immediately with mixed salad greens and lemon wedges.

1
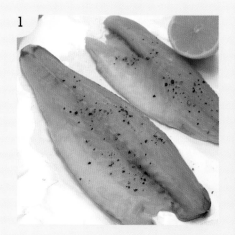

2

2

Sea Bass with Olive Gremolata

 SERVES 4

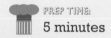 PREP TIME:
5 minutes

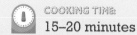 COOKING TIME:
15–20 minutes

nutritional information per serving	460 cal, 17g fat, 2.5g sat fat, 3g total sugars, 0.2g salt

The piquant flavors of lemon, olives, and capers provide the perfect sauce for tasty sea bass.

INGREDIENTS

2 pounds small new potatoes

4 sea bass fillets, about 6 ounces each

1 tablespoon olive oil

¼ cup dry white wine

salt and pepper

lemon wedges, to serve

olive gremolata

grated rind of 1 lemon

1 garlic clove, chopped

2 large handfuls flat-leaf parsley (about 2 ounces)

¾ cup pitted ripe black olives

2 tablespoons capers

2 tablespoons olive oil

1. Cook the potatoes in a saucepan of lightly salted boiling water for 15–20 minutes, or until tender.

2. Meanwhile, make the gremolata. Put the lemon rind, garlic, parsley, olives, capers, and oil in a food processor or blender and process briefly to form a coarse paste.

3. Brush the sea bass with the oil and season with salt and pepper. Heat a heavy skillet and cook the sea bass for 5–6 minutes, turning once.

4. Remove the fish from the skillet and keep warm. Stir the wine into the skillet and boil for 1 minute, stirring. Add the gremolata to the skillet and stir for a few seconds to heat gently.

5. Drain the potatoes when tender and crush lightly with a wooden spoon or vegetable masher.

6. Transfer the sea bass and crushed potatoes to warm serving plates and serve immediately with the gremolata and lemon wedges.

4

5

GOES WELL WITH *Seasonal vegetables would go perfectly with this dish.*

Monkfish with a Lemon & Parsley Crust

 SERVES 4

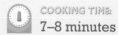 PREP TIME:
5 minutes

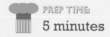 COOKING TIME:
7–8 minutes

nutritional information per serving	244 cal, 12g fat, 1.5g sat fat, 0.5g total sugars, 0.4g salt

Monkfish is available all year round, and the firm, meaty flesh makes it the ideal choice for recipes with robust flavors. However, this simple lemon and parsley topping shows how adaptable it is.

INGREDIENTS

¼ cup sunflower oil

¼ cup fresh bread crumbs

¼ cup chopped fresh parsley, plus extra sprigs to garnish

finely grated rind of 1 large lemon

4 monkfish fillets, about 5–6 ounces each

salt and pepper

1. Preheat the oven to 350°F. Put the oil, bread crumbs, parsley, and lemon rind in a large mixing bowl. Season with salt and pepper and mix together.

2. Arrange the fish fillets in a large, roasting pan. Divide the bread-crumb mixture among the fish and press it down with your fingers to make sure it covers the fillets.

3. Bake in the preheated oven for 7–8 minutes, or until the fish is cooked all the way through.

4. Transfer to warm serving plates. Garnish with parsley sprigs and serve immediately.

1

2
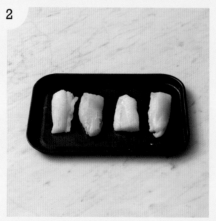

2

GOES WELL WITH
Serve simply with
buttery mashed
potatoes and
fresh peas.

Rustic Fish Casserole

 SERVES 4    PREP TIME:
10 minutes   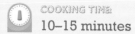 COOKING TIME:
10–15 minutes

nutritional information
per serving   230 cal, 8g fat, 1g sat fat, 6g total sugars, 1.4g salt

*A bowl of steaming fish stew with fresh crusty bread
is a healthy meal that you will want to repeat.*

INGREDIENTS

10 ounces clams, scrubbed
2 tablespoons olive oil
1 large onion, chopped
2 garlic cloves, crushed
2 celery sticks, sliced
12 ounces firm white fish fillet,
such as halibut, sole,
or red snapper
8 ounces prepared squid rings
1¾ cups fish stock
6 plum tomatoes, chopped
small bunch of fresh thyme
salt and pepper
crusty bread, to serve

1. Discard any clams with broken shells and any that refuse to close when tapped.

2. Heat the oil in a large skillet over medium heat. Add the onion, garlic, and celery and cook, stirring occasionally, for 3–4 minutes, until softened but not browned. Meanwhile, cut the fish into chunks.

3. Stir the fish and squid into the skillet, then sauté gently for 2 minutes. Stir in the stock, tomatoes, and thyme, and season with salt and pepper. Cover and simmer gently for 3–4 minutes. Add the clams, cover, and cook over high heat for an additional 2 minutes, or until the shells open. Discard any that remain closed.

4. Transfer to warm serving bowls and serve immediately with crusty bread.

2

3

3

Quick & Creamy Fish Gratin

 SERVES 4    PREP TIME: 5 minutes   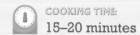 COOKING TIME: 15–20 minutes

nutritional information per serving	522 cal, 24g fat, 13g sat fat, 3g total sugars, 1.7g salt

Although this fish dish is quick and easy to prepare, it makes a good impression served at any dinner table.

INGREDIENTS

1 tablespoon olive oil
2 shallots, finely chopped
⅔ cup white wine or fish stock
1 bay leaf
3 cups thickly sliced white button mushrooms
½ cup crème fraîche or heavy cream
1 pound firm white fish fillets, such as halibut, sole, or red snapper, cut into chunks
6 ounces cooked, peeled shrimp
1¼ cups frozen peas
3 tablespoons butter, melted
3 cups fresh white bread crumbs
salt and pepper
chopped fresh parsley, to garnish

1. Preheat the broiler to medium. Heat the oil in an ovenproof saucepan or a shallow flameproof casserole dish and sauté the shallots. Cook for 2–3 minutes, stirring occasionally, until softened. Add the wine, bay leaf, and mushrooms and simmer for 2 minutes, stirring occasionally.

2. Stir in the crème fraîche and add the fish. Season with salt and pepper. Bring to a boil, cover, and simmer for 5–6 minutes, until the fish is almost cooked.

3. Remove and discard the bay leaf, add the shrimp and peas, and bring back to a boil.

4. Meanwhile, re-melt the butter in a separate saucepan, if necessary, and stir in the bread crumbs. Spread the bread crumb mixture evenly over the top of the fish mixture.

5. Place the saucepan under the preheated broiler for 3–4 minutes, until the topping is golden brown and bubbling.

6. Transfer to warm serving plates. Garnish with parsley and serve immediately.

Grilled Salmon Steak with Noodles

PREP TIME:
5 minutes

COOKING TIME:
6–8 minutes

nutritional information
per serving · 578 cal, 28g fat, 2g sat fat, 2g total sugars, 1.8g salt

This simple salmon dish has a subtle Asian flavor, warmly spiced with ginger and sesame.

INGREDIENTS

2 tablespoons light soy sauce

1 tablespoon finely grated fresh ginger

4 salmon fillets

sunflower oil, for brushing

8 ounces egg noodles

2 teaspoons sesame oil

1 tablespoon sesame seeds, toasted

lightly stir-fried bok choy and carrot strips, to serve

1. Preheat a ridged grill pan over high heat. Place the soy sauce and ginger in a large mixing bowl. Add the salmon fillets to the mixture and turn to coat.

2. Brush the grill pan with oil. Place the salmon on the pan and cook for 6–8 minutes, turning once, until firm.

3. Meanwhile, cook the noodles in a saucepan of lightly salted boiling water according to the package package, until tender. Drain well and stir in the sesame oil.

4. Transfer the salmon and noodles to warm serving plates. Top with the sesame seeds and serve immediately with the vegetables.

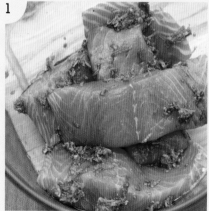

Salmon with Lentil Salad

 SERVES 4    PREP TIME: 5 minutes   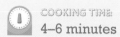 COOKING TIME: 4–6 minutes

nutritional information per serving | 350 cal, 21g fat, 3g sat fat, 2g total sugars, 1.4g salt

Quick to cook and nutritious, fresh salmon is a good choice for easy summertime meals.

INGREDIENTS

1 pound skinless salmon fillet

1 bay leaf

2½ cups fish stock or water

1 (15½-ounce) can lentils, rinsed and drained

4 scallions, thinly sliced

2 tablespoons chopped parsley

3 tablespoons extra-virgin olive oil

juice of 1 lemon

handful of arugula

salt and pepper

1. Put the salmon and bay leaf in a wide saucepan and pour the stock over the fish. Bring to a boil, then reduce the heat, cover, and simmer gently for 4–6 minutes, depending on thickness, until the fish flakes easily. Drain well.

2. Put the lentils, scallions, and parsley in a large mixing bowl and mix together. Put the oil and lemon juice in a separate bowl. Season with salt and pepper and mix together. Stir half the oil and lemon juice dressing into the lentils.

3. Divide the arugula among serving plates and top with the lentil mixture. Flake the salmon over the arugula and drizzle with the remaining dressing. Serve immediately.

**GOES WELL
WITH**
Baby new potatoes,
boiled with a sprig of
mint and tossed with
a pat of butter, make
the perfect partner
for the salmon
and lentils.

Smoked Salmon with Tagliatelle

 SERVES 4    PREP TIME: 5 minutes   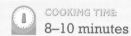 COOKING TIME: 8–10 minutes

nutritional information per serving	410 cal, 10g fat, 1.5g sat fat, 2g total sugars, 1g salt

By adding smoked salmon to a simple pasta dish, you immediately create something special.

INGREDIENTS

12 ounces dried tagliatelle

2 tablespoons olive oil

1 garlic clove, finely chopped

4 ounces smoked salmon, cut into thin strips

3 cups arugula

salt and pepper

1. Bring a large, saucepan of lightly salted water to a boil. Add the pasta, bring back to a boil, and cook according to the package directions, until tender but still firm to the bite.

2. Meanwhile, heat the oil in a large skillet over low heat. Add the garlic and cook, stirring continuously, for 1 minute.

3. Add the salmon and arugula. Season with pepper and cook, stirring continuously, for 1 minute. Remove the skillet from the heat.

4. Drain the pasta and combine with the smoked salmon-and-arugula mixture. Transfer to warm serving plates and serve immediately.

1

2

3

Farfalle with Salmon & Vegetables

 SERVES 2  PREP TIME: 5 minutes  COOKING TIME: 15–20 minutes

nutritional information per serving	774 cal, 44g fat, 17g sat fat, 6g total sugars, 0.3g salt

Farfalle is more familiarly called bow-tie pasta, although it actually comes from the Italian word that means "butterfly."

INGREDIENTS

pared zest of 1 lemon, plus 1 tablespoon lemon juice

1 tablespoon olive oil, plus extra for brushing

8 ounces asparagus, trimmed

1 large zucchini, thinly sliced on the diagonally

8 ounces salmon fillet

6 ounces dried farfalle (bow-tie pasta)

½ cup crème fraîche or heavy cream

2 cups baby spinach

salt and pepper

1. Preheat a ridged grill pan until hot.

2. Mix together the lemon juice and olive oil. Add the asparagus and zucchini. Season with salt and pepper and toss together. Cook the vegetables in batches in the grill pan for 2–3 minutes on each side, until tender. Set aside and keep warm.

3. Brush the grill pan with oil. Place the salmon in the pan and cook for 6–8 minutes, turning once, until firm. Cut into bite-size pieces, set aside, and keep warm.

4. Meanwhile, bring a large saucepan of lightly salted water to a boil. Add the pasta, bring back to a boil, and cook according to the package directions, until tender but still firm to the bite. Drain, set aside, and keep warm.

5. Heat the crème fraîche and lemon zest in the pasta saucepan until melted. Add the baby spinach to the pan, followed by the pasta, chargrilled vegetables, and salmon pieces. Season with salt and pepper and mix together.

6. Transfer to warm serving plates and serve immediately.

Spicy Tuna Fish Cakes

 SERVES 4

 PREP TIME: 5 minutes

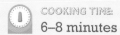 COOKING TIME: 6–8 minutes

nutritional information per serving	306 cal, 18g fat, 3.5g sat fat, 1g total sugars, 0.7g salt

The addition of curry paste to the fish cake mixture in this recipe is perfect with the tuna and makes this a recipe the family will love.

INGREDIENTS

1 (5-ounce) can chunk light tuna in oil, drained

1 cup prepared mashed potatoes

2–3 tablespoons curry paste

1 scallion, trimmed and finely chopped

1 egg, beaten

¼ cup all-purpose flour, plus extra for shaping

sunflower oil or peanut oil, for pan-frying

salt and pepper

arugula and lemon wedges, to serve

1. Put the tuna in a large mixing bowl. Add the mashed potatoes, curry paste, scallion, and egg. Season with salt and pepper and mix together.

2. Divide the mixture into four portions and shape each into a ball. Then, on a floured surface, flatten slightly to make a patty shape of your preferred thickness. Season the flour with salt and pepper. Dust each patty in the seasoned flour.

3. Heat the oil in a large skillet, add the patties, and cook for 3–4 minutes on each side, until crisp and golden.

4. Transfer to warm serving plates and serve immediately with arugula and lemon wedges.

GOES WELL WITH

Serve boiled rice and
an Indian chutney
or raita with the
fish cakes, or slip
them into warm pita
bread filled with
arugula and a
little mayonnaise.

Pasta with Tuna & Olives

 SERVES 4    PREP TIME: 15 minutes   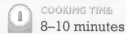 COOKING TIME: 8–10 minutes

nutritional information per serving	584 kcal , 26g fat, 10g sat fat, 2g total sugars, 0.8g salt

If you like the pungent flavor of olives and capers, this super-speedy dish is just for you.

INGREDIENTS

12 ounces dried conchiglie (pasta shells)

¼ cup olive oil

4 tablespoons butter

3 large garlic cloves, thinly sliced

1 (5-ounce) can chunk light tuna in oil, drained

2 tablespoons lemon juice

1 tablespoon capers, drained

10–12 ripe black olives, pitted and sliced

2 tablespoons chopped fresh flat-leaf parsley

salt

1. Bring a large saucepan of lightly salted water to a boil. Add the pasta, bring back to a boil, and cook according to the package directions, until tender but still firm to the bite.

2. Meanwhile, heat the oil and half the butter in a large saucepan over medium heat. Add the garlic and cook for a few seconds.

3. Reduce the heat to low. Flake the tuna into smaller pieces using two forks. Add the tuna, lemon juice, capers, and olives. Stir gently until all the ingredients are heated all the way through.

4. Drain the pasta and combine with the tuna mixture. Add the parsley and remaining butter and toss well to mix. Transfer to warm serving plates and serve immediately.

Grilled Tuna with Lemon, Capers & Thyme

 SERVES 4   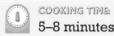 PREP TIME: 5 minutes   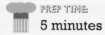 COOKING TIME: 5–8 minutes

nutritional information
per serving   339 cal, 19g fat, 4g sat fat, 0g total sugars, 1g salt

You need a ridged grill pan to cook this recipe so the tuna will remain juicy and firm. It will also create the attractive stripes on the fish, making a quick and easy recipe for tuna steaks look special.

INGREDIENTS

4 tuna steaks,
about 6 ounces each

¼ cup olive oil

finely grated rind and juice
of 1 lemon

3 tablespoons capers, rinsed

2 tablespoons chopped
fresh thyme

salt and pepper

lemon wedges, to serve

1. Brush the tuna steaks with 1 tablespoon of the oil and season with salt and pepper.

2. Put the remaining oil, the lemon rind and juice, capers, and thyme in a small saucepan over low heat.

3. Heat a ridged grill pan until hot, then cook the tuna, in batches if necessary, for 2–3 minutes on each side.

4. Bring the lemon and caper mixture to a boil and spoon over the tuna.

5. Transfer to warm serving plates and serve immediately with lemon wedges.

1

2

4

GOES WELL WITH
Plain, boiled new
potatoes and steamed
broccoli with a yogurt
dressing make a good
healthy accompaniment.

Tuna Noodle Casserole

 SERVES 4
 PREP TIME: 10 minutes
 COOKING TIME: 20–25 minutes

nutritional information **per serving** | 731 cal, 39g fat, 20g sat fat, 3.5g total sugars, 1.7g salt

This is an easy dish that's perfect for a weekday meal. If you don't have any cream, you can replace it with milk.

INGREDIENTS

8 ounces dried macaroni

1 (12-ounce) can chunk light tuna in oil, drained and flaked

1 small red onion, grated

2 tablespoons chopped parsley

1¾ cups shredded cheddar cheese

1 extra-large egg, beaten

1 cup light cream

¼ teaspoon grated nutmeg

salt and pepper

mixed green salad, to serve

1. Preheat the oven to 425°F. Place a baking sheet on the middle shelf to heat. Cook the macaroni in lightly salted boiling water according to the package directions, until tender but still firm to the bite. Drain.

2. Place the macaroni, tuna, onion, parsley, and half the cheese in a large mixing bowl. Mix together. Spread evenly in a shallow, 2-quart casserole dish.

3. Put the egg, cream, and nutmeg in a mixing bowl. Season with salt and pepper and mix together. Pour the sauce over the macaroni mixture and sprinkle with the remaining cheese.

4. Place the dish on the preheated baking sheet in the oven and bake for about 15 minutes, until golden brown and bubbling.

5. Transfer to warm serving plates and serve immediately with a mixed green salad.

SOMETHING
DIFFERENT
Try replacing
the tuna with
canned red salmon
for a more
luxurious dish.

Quick Paella

nutritional information per serving	385 cal, 12g fat, 3.5g sat fat, 5g total sugars, 2.8g salt

Paella is usually a time-consuming dish, but this simpler version is ready in less than half an hour!

INGREDIENTS

2 tablespoons olive oil

1 onion, thinly sliced

1 red bell pepper, sliced

4 ounces chorizo, sliced

1 cup long-grain rice

3½ cups boiling fish stock

pinch of saffron threads

1 cup frozen peas

8 ounces cooked, peeled jumbo shrimp

salt and pepper

chopped fresh flat-leaf parsley, to garnish

crusty bread, to serve

1. Heat the oil in a large saucepan over medium heat. Add the onion and red bell pepper and cook for 2 minutes, stirring continously. Stir in the chorizo and rice and cook for an additional 1 minute.

2. Add the stock and saffron and bring to a boil. Reduce the heat, cover the pan, and simmer, stirring occasionally, for 10 minutes, until the rice is almost tender.

3. Stir in the peas and shrimp and season with salt and pepper, then cover and cook gently for an additional 4–5 minutes, until the rice is tender.

4. Transfer to warm serving plates. Garnish with parsley and serve immediately with crusty bread.

COOKS' NOTE
If you don't have
fish stock, use
chicken stock or
vegetable stock in-
stead, or you can
use a bouillon cube
or bouillon granules.

Spicy Thai Seafood Stew

 SERVES 4   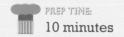 PREP TIME: 10 minutes   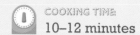 COOKING TIME: 10–12 minutes

nutritional information per serving	623 cal, 28g fat, 19g sat fat, 1g total sugars, 1.4g salt

The list of ingredients in this recipe may seem long, but once you have them all assembled, the cooking is done in minutes and the result is certainly worth the effort.

INGREDIENTS

1 cup long-grain rice

8 ounces squid, cleaned and tentacles discarded

1 pound firm white fish fillets, such as monkfish, halibut, or red snapper

1 tablespoon vegetable oil

4 shallots, finely chopped

2 garlic cloves, finely chopped

2 tablespoons Thai green curry paste

2 small lemongrass stalks, finely chopped

1 teaspoon shrimp paste

2 cups coconut milk

8 ounces jumbo shrimp, peeled and deveined

12 clams, scrubbed

8 fresh basil leaves, finely shredded, plus extra leaves to garnish

1. Cook the rice in a saucepan of lightly salted water according to the package directions, until tender. Drain.

2. Meanwhile, using a sharp knife, cut the squid into thick rings and cut the fish into bite-size chunks.

3. Preheat a wok or large skillet over high heat. Add the oil and heat until hot. Add the shallots, garlic, and curry paste and stir-fry for 1–2 minutes.

4. Add the lemongrass and shrimp paste, then stir in the coconut milk and bring to a boil.

5. Reduce the heat until the liquid is simmering gently, then add the squid, fish, and shrimp and simmer for 2 minutes.

6. Discard any clams with broken shells and any that refuse to close when tapped. Add the clams and simmer for an additional minute, or until the clams have opened. Discard any that remain closed. Sprinkle the shredded basil leaves over the stew.

7. Transfer to warm serving bowls. Garnish with basil leaves and serve immediately with the rice.

Seafood Risotto

 SERVES 4    PREP TIME: 10 minutes   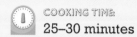 COOKING TIME: 25–30 minutes

nutritional information per serving	688 cal, 19g fat, 8g sat fat, 1.5g total sugars, 1.8g salt

A risotto such as this one is great for entertaining and will really impress your guests.

INGREDIENTS

⅔ cup dry white wine

4 baby squid, cleaned and sliced

8 ounces shrimp, peeled and deveined

8 ounces mussels, scrubbed and debearded

2 tablespoons olive oil

4 tablespoons butter

1 onion, finely chopped

2 garlic cloves, finely chopped

2 bay leaves

1¾ cups risotto rice

about 6½ cups hot fish stock

salt and pepper

chopped fresh flat-leaf parsley, to garnish

1. Heat the wine in a large saucepan over medium heat. Add the squid and shrimp, cover, and cook for 2 minutes. Remove the squid and shrimp with a slotted spoon and set aside.

2. Discard any mussels with broken shells and any that refuse to close when tapped. Add the mussels to the pan, cover, and cook for 2–3 minutes, until they have opened. Discard any that remain closed. Drain the mussels, reserving the juices, and remove from their shells.

3. Heat the oil and butter in a large saucepan over medium heat. Add the onion and cook, stirring frequently, for 3–4 minutes, until softened.

4. Add the garlic, bay leaves, and rice, then mix to coat in the butter and oil. Cook, stirring continuously, for 2–3 minutes, until the grains are translucent.

5. Stir in the cooking juices from the mussels, then gradually add the hot stock, a ladleful at a time. Cook, stirring, for 15 minutes, until the liquid is absorbed and the rice is creamy.

6. Stir in the cooked seafood, cover, and cook for an additional 2 minutes to heat all the way through. Remove and discard the bay leaves. Season with salt and pepper.

7. Transfer to warm serving plates. Garnish with parsley and serve immediately.

Mixed Seafood Pasta

 SERVES 4   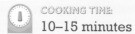 PREP TIME: 10 minutes   COOKING TIME: 10–15 minutes

nutritional information per serving	795 cal, 41g fat, 20g sat fat, 3g total sugars, 1.3g salt

This is a lavish dish that's special enough for an informal dinner party or a weekend family treat.

INGREDIENTS

10 ounces dried conchiglie (pasta shells)

2 tablespoons butter

3 shallots, finely chopped

⅔ cup dry white wine

12 ounces skinless salmon fillet, cut into bite-size pieces

¾ cup heavy cream

2 tablespoons chopped fresh dill, plus extra for garnish

8 ounces peeled cooked shrimp

6 ounces cooked, shelled mussels

salt and pepper

1. Bring a large saucepan of lightly salted water to a boil. Add the pasta, bring back to a boil, and cook according to the package directions, until tender but still firm to the bite.

2. Meanwhile, melt the butter in a large saucepan over medium heat and sauté the shallots, stirring, for 2–3 minutes.

3. Add the wine and salmon, bring to a boil, then reduce the heat, cover, and simmer for 5-6 minutes, until the fish flakes easily. Lift out the salmon and keep warm.

4. Stir in the cream and dill, then add the salmon, shrimp, and mussels. Stir until thoroughly heated and season with salt and pepper. Drain the pasta and combine with the fish and sauce.

5. Transfer to warm serving bowls. Garnish with dill and serve immediately.

2

3

4

COOK'S NOTE
You can replace the salmon, shrimp, and mussels with 2 (14-ounce) packages of frozen seafood mix, defrosted before using. Or use frozen salmon, shrimp, and mussels from separate packages.

Calamari with Shrimp

 SERVES 6   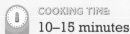 PREP TIME: 5 minutes   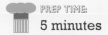 COOKING TIME: 10–15 minutes

nutritional information per serving | 170 cal, 6g fat, 1g sat fat, 1g total sugars, 0.4g salt

In Mediterranean countries, squid is referred to as calamari. You will find it already prepared at the fish counter or in the freezer cabinet.

INGREDIENTS

2 tablespoons olive oil

4 scallions, thinly sliced

2 garlic cloves, finely chopped

1 pound cleaned squid bodies, thickly sliced

½ cup dry white wine

1½ cups fresh or frozen baby fava beans

8 ounces raw jumbo shrimp, peeled and deveined

¼ cup chopped fresh flat-leaf parsley

salt and pepper

crusty bread, to serve

1. Heat the oil in a large skillet over medium heat. Add the scallions and cook over medium heat, stirring occasionally, for 4–5 minutes, until soft.

2. Add the garlic and cook, stirring, for 30 seconds, until soft. Add the squid and cook over high heat, stirring occasionally, for 2 minutes, or until golden brown.

3. Stir in the wine and bring to a boil. Add the beans, reduce the heat, cover, and simmer for 5–8 minutes, if using fresh beans, or 4–5 minutes if using frozen beans, until tender.

4. Add the shrimp, cover, and simmer for an additional 2–3 minutes, until the shrimp turn pink and start to curl. Stir in the parsley and season with salt and pepper. Transfer to warm serving bowls and serve immediately with crusty bread.

1

2

4

BE PREPARED
Prepare all your
ingredients earlier
in the day and
refrigerate them to
save time when you
are ready to cook.

Thai Shrimp Noodle Bowl

 SERVES 4    PREP TIME: 10 minutes    COOKING TIME: 5 minutes

nutritional information per serving	506 cal, 21g fat, 10g sat fat, 5g total sugars, 2g salt

This flavorsome Thai broth is full of all the great fresh tastes of this exotic land.

INGREDIENTS

1 bunch scallions

2 celery sticks

1 red bell pepper

8 ounces rice vermicelli noodles

2 tablespoons peanut oil

⅓ cup unsalted peanuts

1 fresh Thai chile, sliced

1 lemongrass stalk, crushed

1¾ cups fish stock or chicken stock

1 cup coconut milk

2 teaspoons Thai fish sauce

12 ounces cooked, peeled jumbo shrimp

salt and pepper

3 tablespoons chopped fresh cilantro, to garnish

1. Trim the scallions and celery and thinly slice diagonally. Seed and thinly slice the bell pepper.

2. Prepare the noodles according to the package directions, cooking until tender. Drain.

3. Preheat a wok or large skillet over high heat. Add the oil and heat until hot. Add the peanuts and stir-fry for 1–2 minutes, until golden. Lift out with a slotted spoon.

4. Add the sliced vegetables to the wok and stir-fry over high heat for 1–2 minutes. Add the chile, lemongrass, stock, coconut milk, and fish sauce and bring to a boil.

5. Stir in the shrimp and bring back to a boil, stirring. Season with salt and pepper, then add the noodles.

6. Transfer to warm serving bowls. Garnish with cilantro and serve immediately.

Spaghetti with Shrimp & Garlic

 SERVES 4    PREP TIME:
5 minutes    COOKING TIME:
20 minutes

nutritional information
per serving   793 cal, 37g fat, 18g sat fat, 6g total sugars, 0.7g salt

*Garlicky shrimp in a robust tomato sauce will make this
a favorite weekend winner.*

INGREDIENTS

3 tablespoons olive oil

3 tablespoons butter

4 garlic cloves, finely chopped

2 tablespoons seeded and finely
chopped red bell pepper

2 tablespoons tomato paste

½ cup dry white wine

1 pound dried spaghetti

12 ounces peeled and
deveined shrimp

½ cup heavy cream

salt and pepper

3 tablespoons chopped fresh flat-
leaf parsley, to garnish

1. Heat the oil and butter in a saucepan over medium–low heat. Add the garlic and red bell pepper. Sauté for a few seconds, until the garlic is just beginning to color. Stir in the tomato paste and wine. Cook for 10 minutes, stirring continuously.

2. Bring a large, saucepan of lightly salted water to a boil. Add the pasta, bring back to a boil, and cook according to the package directions, until tender but still firm to the bite.

3. Meanwhile, add the shrimp to the sauce and increase the heat to medium–high. Cook for 2 minutes, stirring continuously, until the shrimp turn pink. Reduce the heat and stir in the cream. Cook for 1 minute, stirring continuously, until thickened. Season with salt and pepper. Drain the pasta and combine with the sauce.

4. Transfer the pasta and sauce to warm serving bowls. Garnish with parsley and serve immediately.

1

3

3

BE PREPARED
Make the sauce in
advance and just
reheat. You can also
buy fresh pasta
instead of dried,
which is quicker
to cook.

Tagliatelle with Mussels in White Wine

 SERVES 4

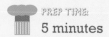 PREP TIME: 5 minutes

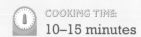 COOKING TIME: 10–15 minutes

nutritional information **per serving** | 747 cal, 18g fat, 9g sat fat, 5g total sugars, 1.5g salt

Fresh mussels take a little bit of preparation, so look out for packaged ones in the supermarket that have had the work done for you.

INGREDIENTS

4½ pounds mussels, scrubbed and debearded

1 large onion, chopped

3 garlic cloves, finely chopped

2 cups dry white wine

1 bay leaf

2 sprigs of fresh thyme

⅓ cup chopped fresh flat-leaf parsley

1 tablespoon chopped fresh rosemary

4 tablespoons butter

1 pound dried tagliatelle or other broad-ribboned pasta

salt and pepper

1. Rinse the mussels well, discarding any with broken shells or that remain open when tapped.

2. Put the onion, garlic, white wine, herbs, and 2 tablespoons of the butter in a saucepan. Bring to a boil, then reduce the heat. Add the mussels, then season with salt and pepper. Cover and cook over medium heat for 3–4 minutes, shaking the pan, until the mussels open. Remove from the heat. Lift out the mussels with a slotted spoon, reserving the liquid. Discard any that remain closed. Remove most of the others from their shells, reserving a few in their shells to garnish. Remove and discard the bay leaf from the liquid.

3. Bring a large, saucepan of lightly salted water to a boil. Add the pasta, bring back to a boil, and cook according to the package directions, until tender but still firm to the bite. Drain the pasta and divide it among individual serving bowls. Spoon the mussels over the pasta. Strain the mussel liquid and return to the pan. Add the remaining butter and heat until melted. Pour over the pasta, garnish with the mussels in their shells, and serve immediately.

Cabbage & Walnut Stir-Fry *218*

Sweet & Sour Tofu with Vegetables *220*

Mushroom Stir-Fry with Noodles *222*

Chile Broccoli Pasta *224*

Pappardelle with Cherry Tomatoes, Arugula & Mozzarella *226*

Spaghetti with Parsley & Parmesan *228*

Macaroni & Double Cheese *230*

Risotto with Peas & Gorgonzola *232*

Cashew Nut Paella *234*

Spicy Bean Chili *236*

Mushroom Fajitas *238*

Mushroom Stroganoff *240*

Mushroom & Cauliflower Cheese Gratin *242*

Bean Burgers *244*

Falafel Burgers *246*

Mushroom Burgers *248*

Quick Ratatouille *250*

Speedy Vegetable Lasagna *252*

Vegetable Pizza *254*

Vegetable Tacos *256*

Cheesy Baked Zucchini *258*

Puff-Topped Vegetable Pie *260*

Vegetable Tortilla *262*

Egg Tortilla with Feta & Corn *264*

Vegetables

Cabbage & Walnut Stir-Fry

 SERVES 4    PREP TIME: 5 minutes   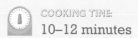 COOKING TIME: 10–12 minutes

nutritional information per serving	409 cal, 35g fat, 5g sat fat, 11g total sugars, 0.2g salt

This is a great stir-fry dish with a variety of tastes and textures that everyone will appreciate.

INGREDIENTS

¼ cup peanut oil

1 tablespoon walnut oil

2 garlic cloves, crushed

3½ cups thinly shredded green cabbage

3½ cups thinly shredded red cabbage

8 scallions, trimmed

1 (8-ounce) package firm tofu, rinsed, drained, and cubed

2 tablespoons lemon juice

¾ cup walnut halves

2 teaspoons Dijon mustard

salt and pepper

2 teaspoons poppy seeds, to garnish

1. Preheat a wok or large skillet over high heat. Add the peanut oil and walnut oil and heat until hot. Add the the garlic, green cabbage, red cabbage, scallions, and tofu and cook for 5 minutes, stirring.

2. Add the lemon juice, walnuts, and mustard to the wok and stir to combine thoroughly.

3. Season the mixture with salt and pepper and cook for an additional 5 minutes, or until the cabbage is tender.

4. Transfer to warm serving bowls. Garnish with poppy seeds and serve immediately.

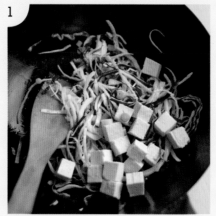

Sweet & Sour Tofu with Vegetables

 SERVES 4   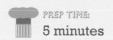 PREP TIME: 5 minutes    COOKING TIME: 8–10 minutes

nutritional information per serving	281cal, 13g fat, 2g sat fat, 14g total sugars, 0.2g salt

This crunchy, colorful stir-fry has a light, tangy sauce that makes it the perfect meat-free dish.

INGREDIENTS

2 tablespoons vegetable oil

2 garlic cloves, crushed

2 celery stalks, thinly sliced

1 carrot, cut into thin strips

1 green bell pepper, diced

1 cup cut snow peas (halved diagonally)

8 baby corn

1 cup bean sprouts

1 (1-pound) package firm tofu, rinsed, drained, and cubed

sauce

2 tablespoons light brown sugar

2 tablespoons wine vinegar

1 cup vegetable stock

1 teaspoon tomato paste

1 tablespoon cornstarch

1. Preheat a wok or large skillet over high heat. Add the oil and heat until hot. Add the garlic, celery, carrot, bell pepper, snow peas, and baby corn and stir-fry for 3–4 minutes.

2. Add the bean sprouts and tofu to the wok and cook for 2 minutes, stirring frequently.

3. To make the sauce, put the sugar, wine vinegar, stock, tomato paste, and cornstarch in a large bowl. Mix together. Stir into the wok, bring to a boil, and cook, stirring continously, until the sauce thickens. Continue to cook for 1 minute.

4. Transfer to warm serving bowls and serve immediately.

Mushroom Stir-Fry with Noodles

 SERVES 4    PREP TIME: 5 minutes   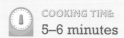 COOKING TIME: 5–6 minutes

nutritional information per serving	410 cal, 18g fat, 3.5g sat fat, 7g total sugars, 0.5g salt

This is a speedy Asian-style dish that's suitable for vegetarians and satisfying for meat-eaters, too.

INGREDIENTS

8 ounces medium egg noodles

2–3 tablespoons sunflower oil

1 clove garlic, finely chopped

¾-inch piece ginger, finely chopped

1 bunch scallions, chopped, plus some longer pieces, to garnish

handful of baby spinach

4 cups sliced white button mushrooms,

8 ounces shiitake mushrooms, sliced

3 tablespoons dry sherry

⅓ cup hoisin sauce

½ cup cashew nuts, toasted, to garnish

salt and pepper

1. Cook the noodles in a saucepan of lightly salted boiling water according to the package directions, until tender. Drain well.

2. Preheat a wok or large skillet over high heat. Add the oil and heat until hot. Add the garlic, ginger, and scallions for 30 seconds. Add the spinach and stir until just wilted.

3. Add the mushrooms and stir-fry for 2–3 minutes to soften. Stir in the sherry and hoisin sauce, then stir-fry for an additional 2–3 minutes, until the mushrooms are cooked. Stir in the noodles and season with salt and pepper.

4. Transfer to warm serving bowls. Garnish with cashew nuts and scallions and serve immediately.

Chile Broccoli Pasta

 SERVES 4 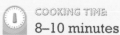 PREP TIME: 5 minutes  COOKING TIME: 8–10 minutes

nutritional information per serving	300 cal, 10g fat, 1.6g sat fat, 3g total sugars, trace salt

Be careful to avoid touching your eyes or any sensitive areas after you've chopped chiles—they will sting.

INGREDIENTS

8 ounces dried macaroni

3 cups broccoli florets

¼ cup extra virgin olive oil

2 large garlic cloves, chopped

2 fresh red chiles, seeded and diced

8 cherry tomatoes

salt

handful of fresh basil leaves, to garnish

1. Bring a large saucepan of lightly salted water to a boil. Add the pasta, bring back to a boil, and cook according to the package directions, until tender but still firm to the bite. Drain the pasta, refresh under cold running water, and drain again. Set aside.

2. Meanwhile, bring a separate saucepan of lightly salted water to a boil, add the broccoli, and cook for 5 minutes. Drain, refresh under cold running water, and drain again.

3. Heat the oil in a large skillet over medium heat. Add the garlic, chiles, and tomatoes and cook, stirring continuously, for 1 minute.

4. Add the broccoli and mix well. Cook for 2 minutes, stirring, to heat through. Add the pasta and mix again. Cook for an additional minute.

5. Transfer to warm serving plates. Garnish with basil leaves and serve immediately.

2

3

4

Pappardelle with Cherry Tomatoes, Arugula & Mozzarella

 SERVES 4

 PREP TIME:
5 minutes

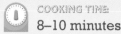 COOKING TIME:
8–10 minutes

nutritional information per serving	610 cal, 23g fat, 11.5g sat fat, 5g total sugars, 0.8g salt

The broad pasta noodle known as pappardelle is often served with robust game stews. It's a wider version of tagliatelle, which you may prefer to use instead.

INGREDIENTS

1 pound dried pappardelle
2 tablespoons olive oil
1 garlic clove, chopped
2½ cups halved cherry tomatoes
5 cups arugula
10 ounces mozzarella, chopped
salt and pepper
grated Parmesan cheese, to serve

1. Bring a large saucepan of lightly salted water to a boil. Add the pasta, bring back to a boil, and cook according to the package directions, until tender but still firm to the bite.

2. Meanwhile, heat the oil in a skillet over medium heat and sauté the garlic, stirring, for 1 minute, without browning.

3. Add the tomatoes, season well with salt and pepper, and cook gently for 2–3 minutes, until softened.

4. Drain the pasta and stir into the skillet. Add the arugula and mozzarella, then stir until the leaves wilt.

5. Transfer to warm serving bowls and serve immediately with Parmesan cheese.

1

3

4

Spaghetti with Parsley & Parmesan

SERVES 4

PREP TIME: 5 minutes

COOKING TIME: 8–10 minutes

nutritional information per serving	605 cal, 35g fat, 22.5g sat fat, 2.5g total sugars, 0.6g salt

You can't find a recipe for a great-tasting pasta dish that's simpler than this one. It's bound to become a favorite for a midweek dinner, served simply with crusty bread and a salad.

INGREDIENTS

1 pound dried spaghetti

1½ sticks unsalted butter

¼ cup chopped fresh flat-leaf parsley

2¼ cups grated Parmesan cheese

salt

crusty bread, to serve

1. Bring a large saucepan of lightly salted water to a boil. Add the pasta, bring back to a boil, and cook according to the package directions, until tender but still firm to the bite. Drain and transfer to a serving dish.

2. Add the butter, parsley, and half the Parmesan cheese and toss well, using 2 forks, until the butter and cheese have melted.

3. Transfer to warm serving bowls and serve immediately with the remaining Parmesan cheese and crusty bread.

1

1

2

Macaroni & Double Cheese

 SERVES 4    PREP TIME: 5 minutes   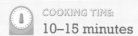 COOKING TIME: 10–15 minutes

nutritional information per serving	540 cal, 31g fat, 12g sat fat, 5g total sugars, 1.5g salt

This is real comfort food and a recipe you'll return to again and again. The combination of two cheeses produces creaminess and a tangy flavor.

INGREDIENTS

8 ounces dried macaroni

9 ounces ricotta cheese

1½ tablespoons whole-grain mustard

3 tablespoons snipped fresh chives, plus extra to garnish

1½ cups halved cherry tomatoes

⅔ cup drained, chopped sun-dried tomatoes in oil

butter or oil, for greasing

1 cup shredded cheddar cheese

salt and pepper

1. Preheat the broiler to high. Bring a large saucepan of lightly salted water to a boil. Add the pasta, bring back to a boil, and cook according to the package directions, until tender but still firm to the bite. Drain.

2. Put the ricotta, mustard, chives, macaroni, cherry tomatoes, and sun-dried tomatoes in a large mixing bowl. Season with salt and pepper and mix together.

3. Grease a 2-quart shallow ovenproof dish. Spoon in the macaroni mixture into the dish, spreading it evenly.

4. Sprinkle the cheddar cheese over the macaroni mixture and cook under the preheated broiler for 4–5 minutes, until golden.

5. Transfer to warm serving plates. Garnish with chives and serve immediately.

2

2

4

Risotto with Peas & Gorgonzola

 SERVES 4 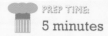 PREP TIME: 5 minutes 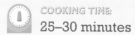 COOKING TIME: 25–30 minutes

nutritional information per serving	658 cal, 25g fat, 12g sat fat, 4g total sugars, 1.7g salt

Gorgonzola is one of Italy's finest cheeses. It's perfect in a risotto, as you will discover when you try this easy recipe.

INGREDIENTS

2 tablespoons olive oil
2 tablespoons butter
1 onion, finely chopped
1 garlic clove, finely chopped
1¾ cups risotto rice
⅔ cup dry white wine
5½ cups hot vegetable stock
2½ cups frozen peas
1⅓ cups crumbled Gorgonzola cheese or other blue cheese
2 tablespoons chopped fresh mint
salt and pepper

1. Heat the oil and butter in a large saucepan over medium heat. Add the onion and cook, stirring frequently, for 3–4 minutes, until softened.

2. Add the garlic and rice and mix to coat in the butter and oil. Cook, stirring continuously, for 2–3 minutes, or until the grains are translucent. Add the wine and cook, stirring continuously, for 1 minute, until reduced.

3. Gradually add the hot stock, a ladleful at a time. Cook, stirring, for 15 minutes, then stir in the peas and cook for an additional 5 minutes, until the liquid is absorbed and the rice is creamy.

4. Remove from the heat. Stir in the Gorgonzola and mint, then season with salt and pepper.

5. Transfer to warm serving bowls and serve immediately.

COOK'S NOTE Continuous stirring is the only way to create the authentic creaminess of a good risotto.

Cashew Nut Paella

 SERVES 4    PREP TIME: 10 minutes   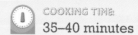 COOKING TIME: 35–40 minutes

nutritional information
per serving   419 cal, 22g fat, 5g sat fat, 8.5g total sugars, 0.2g salt

*Crammed with flavor, this vegetable paella with
the added crunch of cashew nuts is a healthy version
of a Spanish favorite.*

INGREDIENTS

2 tablespoons olive oil

1 tablespoon butter

1 red onion, chopped

¾ cup risotto rice

1 teaspoon ground turmeric

1 teaspoon ground cumin

½ teaspoon chili powder

3 garlic cloves, crushed

1 fresh green chile,
seeded and sliced

1 green bell pepper,
seeded and diced

1 red bell pepper,
seeded and diced

6 baby corn, halved lengthwise

2 tablespoons pitted
ripe black olives

1 large tomato, seeded and diced

2 cups vegetable stock

¾ cup unsalted cashew nuts

⅓ cup frozen peas

2 tablespoons chopped
fresh parsley

pinch of cayenne pepper

salt and pepper

1. Heat the oil and butter in a large skillet over medium heat until the butter has melted.

2. Add the onion and cook, stirring continuously, for 2–3 minutes, until softened.

3. Stir in the rice, turmeric, cumin, chili powder, garlic, chile, green bell pepper, red bell pepper, baby corn, olives, and tomato and cook over medium heat, stirring occasionally, for 5 minutes. Season with salt and pepper.

4. Pour in the stock and bring the mixture to a boil. Reduce the heat and cook gently, stirring continuously, for an additional 20 minutes.

5. Add the cashew nuts and peas and continue to cook, stirring occasionally, for an additional 5 minutes. Season with salt and pepper and add the parsley and cayenne pepper.

6. Transfer to warm serving plates and serve immediately.

Spicy Bean Chili

 SERVES 4    PREP TIME: 5 minutes    COOKING TIME: 15 minutes

nutritional information per serving	180 cal, 6.5g fat, 1g sat fat, 9g total sugars, 0.5g salt

We've combined two types of beans in this meatless chili to provide added texture and flavor.

INGREDIENTS

2 tablespoons olive oil

1 large onion, chopped

1 large green bell pepper, seeded and chopped

2 garlic cloves, crushed

2 teaspoons dried crushed chiles

1 (14½-ounce) can diced tomatoes

1½ cups drained, rinsed canned red kidney beans

1½ cups drained, rinsed canned cannellini beans,

3 tablespoons chopped cilantro

salt and pepper

tortilla chips, to serve

1. Heat the oil in a large skillet over medium heat. Add the onion and green bell pepper and stir-fry for 8 minutes, stirring frequently until softened and lightly browned.

2. Stir in the garlic and chiles, then add the tomatoes and simmer for 2 minutes.

3. Add the beans and cilantro, heat until boiling, then simmer for 5 minutes. Season with salt and pepper.

4. Transfer to warm serving bowls and serve immediately with tortilla chips.

Mushroom Fajitas

SERVES 4

PREP TIME: 10 minutes

COOKING TIME: 10–12 minutes

nutritional information per serving	423 cal, 8g fat, 1g sat fat, 10g total sugars, 0.9g salt

Warm tortillas filled with herb-flavored mushrooms make a great meat-free meal.

INGREDIENTS

2 tablespoons oil

1 pound large flat mushrooms, sliced

1 onion, sliced

1 red bell pepper, seeded and sliced

1 green bell pepper, seeded and sliced

1 garlic clove, crushed

¼–½ teaspoon cayenne pepper

juice and grated rind of 2 limes

2 teaspoons sugar

1 teaspoon dried oregano

8 flour tortillas

salt and pepper

salsa, to serve

1. Heat the oil in a large skillet over medium heat. Add the mushrooms, onion, red bell pepper, green bell pepper, and garlic and cook for 8–10 minutes, until the vegetables are cooked.

2. Add the cayenne pepper, lime juice and rind, sugar, and oregano. Season with salt and pepper and cook for an additional 2 minutes. Remove the vegetables from the skillet, set aside, and keep warm.

3. Clean the skillet. Add the tortillas and warm for a few seconds. Remove from the skillet.

4. Divide the mushroom mixture among the tortillas. Fold the sides over and serve immediately with salsa.

Mushroom Stroganoff

 SERVES 4   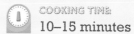 PREP TIME: 5 minutes   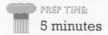 COOKING TIME: 10–15 minutes

nutritional information per serving	213 cal, 21g fat, 14g sat fat, 3g total sugars, 0.2g salt

This dish is considered a Russian specialty, although many countries have added their own flavor to make it unique. This version has no meat but the crème fraîche and paprika certainly add an authentic flavoring.

INGREDIENTS

2 tablespoons butter

1 onion, finely chopped

6½ cups quarted white button mushrooms (about 1 pound)

1 teaspoon tomato paste

1 teaspoon coarse-grain mustard

⅔ cup crème fraîche

1 teaspoon paprika, plus extra to garnish

salt and pepper

fresh flat-leaf parsley sprigs, to garnish

1. Heat the butter in a large skillet over medium heat. Add the onion and cook gently for 5–10 minutes, until soft.

2. Add the mushrooms to the skillet and stir-fry for a few minutes, until they begin to soften. Stir in the tomato paste and mustard, then add the crème fraîche. Cook gently, stirring continuously, for 5 minutes.

3. Stir in the paprika and season with salt and pepper.

4. Transfer to warm serving plates. Garnish with extra paprika and parsley sprigs and serve immediately.

Mushroom & Cauliflower Cheese Gratin

 SERVES 4   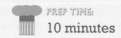 PREP TIME: 10 minutes    COOKING TIME: 20–25 minutes

nutritional information per serving	350 cal, 21g fat, 12g sat fat, 5g total sugars, 1g salt

Mushrooms add an extra dimension to a simple cauliflower dish, which is always a favorite comfort food on its own, or when served as a side dish.

INGREDIENTS

1 cauliflower, cut into florets
4 tablespoons butter
1½ cups sliced white button mushrooms,
salt and pepper

topping

1 cup dry bread crumbs
2 tablespoons grated Parmesan cheese
1 teaspoon dried oregano
1 teaspoon dried parsley
2 tablespoons butter

1. Bring a large saucepan of lightly salted water to a boil. Add the cauliflower and cook for 3 minutes. Remove from the heat, drain well, and transfer to a shallow ovenproof dish.

2. Preheat the oven to 450°F. Melt the butter in a small skillet over medium heat. Add the mushrooms, stir, and cook gently for 3 minutes.

3. Remove from the heat and spoon the mushrooms on top of the cauliflower. Season with salt and pepper.

4. To make the topping, put the bread crumbs, Parmesan cheese, and herbs in a small mixing bowl. Mix together. Sprinkle the topping over the vegetables.

5. Dice the butter and dot over the bread-crumb mixture. Bake in the preheated oven for 15 minutes, or until the topping is golden brown.

6. Transfer to warm serving plates and serve immediately.

Bean Burgers

 SERVES 4    PREP TIME: 10 minutes   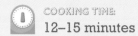 COOKING TIME: 12–15 minutes

nutritional information per serving	351 cal, 10g fat, 2g sat fat, 5.5g total sugars, 1.8g salt

Here's a great-tasting vegetarian burger that is easy to make—and it will certainly impress your guests!

INGREDIENTS

1 tablespoon sunflower oil, plus extra for brushing

1 onion, finely chopped

1 garlic clove, finely chopped

1 teaspoon ground coriander

1 teaspoon ground cumin

1½ cups finely chopped white button mushrooms

1 (15-ounce) can cranberry beans or red kidney beans, drained and rinsed

2 tablespoons chopped fresh flat-leaf parsley

all-purpose flour, for dusting

salt and pepper

hamburger buns and salad greens, to serve

1. Preheat the broiler to high. Heat the oil in a large skillet over medium heat. Add the onion and cook, stirring frequently, for 5 minutes, or until softened. Add the garlic, coriander, and cumin and cook, stirring, for an additional minute. Add the mushrooms and cook, stirring frequently, for 4–5 minutes, until all the liquid has evaporated. Set aside.

2. Put the beans in a small mixing bowl and mash with a fork. Add the mushroom mixture and parsley. Season with salt and pepper and mix together.

3. Divide the mixture into four portions, dust with flour, and shape each into a ball, then flatten slightly to make a patty shape of your preferred thickness. Brush lightly with the oil.

4. Cook the patties under the preheated broiler for 4–5 minutes. Turn the burgers and cook for an additional 4–5, until cooked all the way through.

5. Place the salad greens on the bottom halves of the buns, top with the burgers, and add the lids. Transfer to serving plates and serve immediately.

1

2

3

Falafel Burgers

 SERVES 4  PREP TIME: 10 minutes 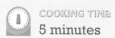 COOKING TIME: 5 minutes

nutritional information per serving	250 cal, 15g fat, 2g sat fat, 1.5g total sugars, 0.7g salt

If you have a food processor or blender, you can quickly pulse the chickpeas to a coarse paste. Otherwise, use a vegetable masher, but it will take a little longer.

INGREDIENTS

1 (29-ounce) can chickpeas, drained and rinsed

1 small onion, chopped

zest and juice of 1 lime

2 teaspoons ground coriander

2 teaspoons ground cumin

all-purpose flour, for dusting

¼ cup olive oil

sprigs fresh basil, to garnish

tomato salsa, to serve

1. Put the chickpeas, onion, lime zest and juice, and the spices into a food processor or blender and process to a coarse paste. Transfer the mixture to a large mixing bowl.

2. Divide the mixture into four portions, dust with flour, and shape each into a ball, then flatten slightly to make a patty shape of your preferred thickness.

3. Heat the oil in a large skillet over medium heat. Add the patties and cook for 2 minutes. Turn over the burgers and cook for an additional 2 minutes, until cooked through and crisp.

4. Transfer to warm serving plates. Garnish with basil sprigs and serve with tomato salsa.

1

2

2

SOMETHING
DIFFERENT
Serve mini versions
of the burgers as
snacks, or stuffed
into warm pita
bread with
salad and a
tahini dressing.

Mushroom Burgers

 SERVES 4    PREP TIME: 10 minutes   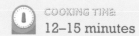 COOKING TIME: 12–15 minutes

nutritional information per serving	409 cal, 15g fat, 3g sat fat, 0.4g total sugars, 1.6g salt

Mushrooms are a good source of fiber, protein, and vitamins, so they're a great meat-free alternative.

INGREDIENTS

1 pound cremini mushrooms
1 onion, quartered
olive oil, for frying
1 garlic clove, crushed
¾ cup dry white bread crumbs
1 medium egg, beaten
1 tablespoon chopped fresh thyme
½ teaspoon ground nutmeg
all-purpose flour, for dusting
salt and pepper

to serve
baby spinach
4 hamburger buns, halved
mayonnaise (optional)

1. Put the mushrooms and onion in a food processor or blender and process until finely chopped.

2. Heat the oil in a large skillet over medium heat. Add the mushrooms and onion and cook for 4–5 minutes, stirring, to evaporate as much moisture as possible. Stir in the garlic and remove from the heat. Transfer the mixture to a large mixing bowl.

3. Add the bread crumbs, egg, thyme, and nutmeg to the bowl. Season with salt and pepper and mix together. Divide the mixture into four portions, dust with flour, and shape each into a ball, then flatten slightly to make a patty shape of your preferred thickness.

4. Wipe the skillet with paper towels. Heat the oil over high heat, add the patties and cook for 4–5 minutes, turning once until cooked through and lightly browned.

5. Place the spinach on the bottom halves of the buns, top with the burgers and a spoonful of mayonnaise, and add the lids. Serve immediately.

Quick Ratatouille

 SERVES 4

 PREP TIME:
10 minutes

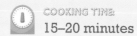 COOKING TIME:
15–20 minutes

nutritional information per serving	162 cal, 12g fat, 2g sat fat, 8g total sugars, 0.1g salt

When cutting up the vegetables, keep all the chunks the same size so that they will cook evenly.

INGREDIENTS

¼ cup olive oil

1 onion, chopped

1 small eggplant, chopped

1 red bell pepper, seeded and chopped

2 zucchini, chopped

2 garlic cloves, chopped

3 tablespoons red wine

1 (14½-ounce) can diced tomatoes

2 bay leaves

salt and pepper

chopped fresh parsley, to garnish

crusty bread, to serve

1. Heat the oil in a large skillet over high heat. Add the onion, eggplant, red bell pepper, and zucchini and cook, stirring, for about 5 minutes, until the vegetables begin to soften.

2. Stir in the garlic, wine, tomatoes, and bay leaves. Bring to a boil, then reduce the heat, cover, and simmer for 10–15 minutes, stirring occasionally, until tender. Remove the bay leaves and season with salt and pepper.

3. Transfer to warm serving plates, garnish with parsley, and serve immediately with crusty bread.

GOES WELL WITH
Add a poached egg
on top and sprinkle
with finely grated
Parmesan cheese.

Speedy Vegetable Lasagna

 SERVES 4  PREP TIME: 5 minutes  COOKING TIME: 10–15 minutes

nutritional information per serving	425 cal, 16g fat, 6g sat fat, 10g total sugars, 0.5g salt

A vegetable lasagna can take hours to make, but these little vegetarian stacks are ready in minutes!

INGREDIENTS

1 red onion, sliced into wedges

1 green bell pepper, seeded and thickly sliced

1 red bell pepper, seeded and thickly sliced

2 large zucchini, sliced diagonally

2 tablespoons olive oil, plus extra for greasing

12 squares of fresh lasagna, about 4 inches across

handful of basil leaves

2 large tomatoes, sliced

1 cup shredded cheddar cheese mozzarella cheese

salt and pepper

mixed salad greens, to serve

1. Preheat the broiler to high. Arrange the onion, green bell pepper, red bell pepper, and zucchini on a baking sheet and drizzle with the oil. Sprinkle with salt and pepper and broil for 6–8 minutes, turning once, until tender.

2. Meanwhile, cook the lasagna squares in a large saucepan of boiling, salted water according to the package directions, until tender. Drain.

3. Place four lasagna squares on a greased baking sheet. Take half the vegetable mixture and divide among the four squares. Top each layer with basil leaves and tomato slices and top with a lasagna square. Divide the remaining vegetable mixture among the four lasagna stacks and then top each with a lasagna square.

4. Sprinkle with the shredded cheese. Cook the lasagna stacks under the preheated broiler for 2 minutes, until the cheese is melted.

5. Transfer to warm serving plates and serve immediately with mixed salad greens.

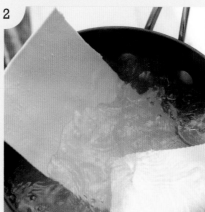

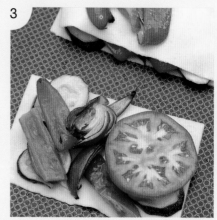

SOMETHING DIFFERENT
For a different look, instead of using squares, use a large, round cookie cutter to stamp out circles from the lasagna sheets.

Vegetable Pizza

 MAKES 1   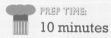 PREP TIME: 10 minutes   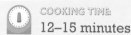 COOKING TIME: 12–15 minutes

nutritional information per pizza	1,187 cal, 56g fat, 17.5g sat fat, 27g total sugars, 2.9g salt

Keep some good-quality, store-bought pizza crusts in the freezer—they're a great standby when time's short.

INGREDIENTS

2 tablespoons olive oil

1 (12-inch) store-bought pizza crust

3 tablespoons tomato paste

1 tablespoon chopped fresh thyme

1 onion, finely chopped

1 small green bell pepper, seeded and thinly sliced

2 tomatoes, sliced

6 pitted ripe black olives, halved

4 ounces mozzarella cheese, torn into pieces

salt and pepper

1. Preheat the oven to 425°F. Brush a large baking sheet with a little oil and place the pizza crust on the sheet.

2. Spread the tomato paste over the pizza crust to within ¾ inch of the edge. Sprinkle with the thyme and arrange the onion, green bell pepper, tomatoes, and olives over the pizza.

3. Sprinkle with the cheese, season with salt and pepper, and drizzle with the remaining oil.

4. Bake in the preheated oven for 12–15 minutes, until bubbling and golden. Serve immediately.

SOMETHING
DIFFERENT

For a change of
flavor, replace the
mozzarella cheese
with crumbled feta
cheese, or pieces
of soft goat cheese.
Try with a
drizzle of chili
oil before serving.

Vegetable Tacos

nutritional information
per serving   337 cal, 20g fat, 6g sat fat, 4g total sugars, 0.7g salt

Quick and easy to make, these handy tacos are a good way to satisfy hungry appetites in a rush.

INGREDIENTS

2 tablespoons olive oil

1 red onion, sliced

2 small zucchini, diced

1 teaspoon ground coriander

½ teaspoon ground cumin

2 tomatoes, chopped

1 (15-ounce) can chickpeas, rinsed and drained

4 taco shells

¾ cup shredded cheddar cheese

salt and pepper

1. Preheat the broiler to high. Heat the oil in a large skillet over medium heat. Add the onion and zucchini and cook for 4–5 minutes, stirring occasionally.

2. Stir in the coriander and cumin, then add the tomatoes and chickpeas. Season with salt and pepper and bring to a boil. Simmer over medium heat, stirring occasionally, for 2 minutes. Spoon the mixture into the taco shells and sprinkle with the cheese.

3. Place on a baking sheet and cook the tacos under the preheated broiler for 1–2 minutes, until the cheese has melted.

4. Transfer to warm serving plates and serve immediately.

COOK'S NOTE
Place pieces of crumpled aluminum foil between the taco shells to hold them upright while adding the filling and cooking under the broiler.

Cheesy Baked Zucchini

 SERVES 4  PREP TIME: 5 minutes  COOKING TIME: 15 minutes

nutritional information
per serving   197 cal, 16g fat, 7g sat fat, 3g total sugars, 0.5g salt

When summer zucchini are plentiful, this is a different way to try serving them. The cheese melts and becomes deliciously gooey.

INGREDIENTS

4 medium zucchini

2 tablespoons extra-virgin olive oil

4 ounces cheddar cheese or mozzarella, thinly sliced

2 large tomatoes, seeded and diced

2 teaspoons fresh basil or oregano, chopped

1. Preheat the oven to 400°F. Slice each zucchini lengthwise into four strips. Brush with oil and place on a large baking sheet.

2. Bake the zucchini in the preheated oven for 10 minutes, without letting them get too soft.

3. Remove the zucchini from the oven. Arrange slices of cheese on top and sprinkle with the diced tomatoes and basil. Return to the oven for 5 minutes, or until the cheese has melted.

4. Transfer to warm serving plates and serve immediately.

1

2

3

Puff-Topped Vegetable Pie

 SERVES 4    PREP TIME:
5 minutes   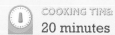 COOKING TIME:
20 minutes

nutritional information
per serving   331 cal, 21g fat, 8.5g sat fat, 5.5g total sugars, 0.6g salt

This easy pie can be made with almost any selection of vegetables, depending on the season.

INGREDIENTS

2 tablespoons olive oil

1 leek, thinly sliced

2 carrots, thinly sliced

3 cups sliced white
button mushrooms

⅔ cup fresh or frozen peas

1 teaspoon dried tarragon

⅔ cup boiling vegetable stock

1 sheet store-bought
ready-to-bake puff pastry

2 tablespoons grated
Parmesan cheese

salt and pepper

boiled new potatoes, to serve

1. Preheat the oven to 425°F and place a baking sheet on the shelf to heat.

2. Heat the oil in a large skillet over high heat. Add the leek and carrots and cook for 2 minutes, stirring occasionally. Add the mushrooms and cook for an additional 2 minutes. Add the peas, tarragon, and stock, then season with salt and pepper. Transfer the mixture to a 1½-quart shallow ovenproof dish.

3. Place the sheet of pastry on top, tucking in any excess around the edges. Make a small slit in the center, brush lightly with a little water, and sprinkle with Parmesan cheese.

4. Place the dish on the baking sheet in the preheated oven and bake for 15 minutes, or until golden brown and well risen.

5. Transfer to warm serving plates and serve immediately with new potatoes.

2

2

3

COOK'S NOTE
Keep a package of
ready-to-bake puffed
pastry in the freezer
for emergencies.
There are normally
two sheets per box,
which is enough to
top two pies.

Vegetable Tortilla

 SERVES 4    PREP TIME: 5 minutes    COOKING TIME: 20–25 minutes

nutritional information per serving	336 cal, 22g fat, 6g sat fat, 4g total sugars, 0.6g salt

This Spanish-style tortilla is good served hot or cold, and it's perfect to pack for picnics.

INGREDIENTS

2 cups peeled, diced potatoes
2 tablespoons olive oil
1 small red onion, sliced
1 red bell pepper, seeded and sliced
6 cherry tomatoes, halved
6 extra-large eggs, beaten
2 tablespoons chopped chives
½ cup grated Parmesan cheese
salt and pepper
mixed salad greens, to serve

1. Preheat the broiler to high. Cook the potatoes in a saucepan of lightly salted water for 8–10 minutes, or until tender. Drain well.

2. Meanwhile, heat the oil in a large ovenproof skillet. Add the onion and bell pepper and cook for 5–6 minutes, stirring occasionally. Stir in the potatoes and tomatoes.

3. Put the eggs, 2 tablespoons of water, and the chives in a large mixing bowl. Season with salt and pepper and beat well. Pour over the vegetables and let cook for 4–5 minutes, until almost set.

4. Sprinkle the Parmesan cheese over the tortilla and cook under the preheated broiler for 2–3 minutes, until bubbling and golden brown.

5. Transfer to warm serving plates. Serve hot or cold with mixed salad greens.

2

3

3

Egg Tortilla with Feta & Corn

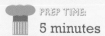 SERVES 4    PREP TIME: 5 minutes    COOKING TIME: 20 minutes

nutritional information per serving	372 cal, 22g fat, 7g sat fat, 6.5g total sugars, 1.5g salt

This is another satisfying recipe that is equally good served hot or cold. It's a tasty alternative to a sandwich in your lunch box.

INGREDIENTS

3 potatoes, cubed
2 tablespoons olive oil
1 onion, chopped
1 zucchini, coarsely shredded
1 (8¾-ounce) can corn, drained
6 eggs
⅔ cup crumbed feta cheese
salt and pepper
paprika, to garnish

1. Preheat the broiler to high. Cook the potatoes in a saucepan of lightly salted boiling water for 5 minutes, or until just tender. Drain well.

2. Heat the oil in a large ovenproof skillet over medium heat. Add the onion and cook for 5 minutes, stirring occasionally, until softened. Add the zucchini and potatoes and cook for 2 minutes. Stir in the corn.

3. Put the eggs in a bowl. Season with salt and pepper and mix together. Pour the eggs over the vegetables, then sprinkle with the feta cheese and cook for 4–5 minutes, until almost set.

4. Cook under the preheated broiler for 2–3 minutes, until bubbling and golden brown. Transfer to warm serving plates. Garnish with paprika and serve hot or cold.

2

3

3

Desserts & Baking

Butterscotch, Mango & Ginger Sundaes

 SERVES 4 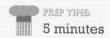 PREP TIME: 5 minutes  COOKING TIME: 5 minutes

nutritional information per serving	1,034 cal, 57g fat, 33g sat fat, 104g total sugars, 0.8g salt

This is a great dessert for when you're in a rush and everyone wants something sweet.

INGREDIENTS

1 large, ripe mango
16 gingersnaps
4 cups vanilla ice cream
2 tablespoons coarsely chopped almonds, toasted

butterscotch sauce

½ cup firmly packed light brown sugar
½ cup light corn syrup
4 tablespoons unsalted butter
½ cup heavy cream
½ teaspoon vanilla extract

1. To make the butterscotch sauce, melt the sugar, light corn syrup, and butter in a small saucepan and simmer for 3 minutes, stirring, until smooth. Stir in the cream and vanilla extract, then remove from the heat.

2. Peel and pit the mango and cut into ½-inch cubes. Place the gingersnaps in a plastic food bag and crush lightly with a rolling pin.

3. Divide half the mango among four sundae glasses and top each with a scoop of the ice cream. Spoon a little of the warm butterscotch sauce over the ice cream and sprinkle with the crushed cookies. Repeat the layers with the remaining ingredients.

4. Sprinkle some of the almonds over the top of each sundae and serve immediately.

1

3

3

COOK'S NOTE

If ripe mangoes are not available, you can use ripe peaches or nectarines as a substitute.

Chocolate Banana Sundae

 SERVES 4    PREP TIME: 10 minutes   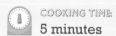 COOKING TIME: 5 minutes

nutritional information **per serving**   804 cal, 51g fat, 27g sat fat, 68g total sugars, 0.4g salt

For a special occasion, nothing beats a filled-to-the-top sundae with ice cream, chocolate sauce, and nuts.

INGREDIENTS

⅔ cup heavy cream

4 bananas, peeled

8 scoops vanilla ice cream

⅔ cup chopped mixed nuts, toasted

⅓ cup grated milk or semisweet dark chocolate

fan-shape wafer cookies, to serve

chocolate sauce

⅓ cup semisweet dark chocolate, broken into pieces

¼ cup light corn syrup

1 tablespoon butter

1 tablespoon brandy or dark rum (optional)

1. To make the chocolate sauce, put the chocolate in a heatproof bowl with the light corn syrup and butter. Set over a saucepan of gently simmering water, stirring, until melted and well combined. Remove the bowl from the heat and stir in the brandy, if using.

2. Whip the cream until just holding its shape and slice the bananas. Place a scoop of ice cream in the bottom of four sundae glasses. Top with half the banana slices and a spoonful of the whipped cream. Spoon a little of the chocolate sauce over the bananas and cream and sprinkle with half the nuts.

3. Repeat the layers with the remaining ingredients, finishing each with a second spoonful of ice cream. Sprinkle any remaining nuts and the grated chocolate over the top of each sundae.

4. Serve immediately with cookies.

1

2

3

COOK'S NOTE
You may not have sundae glasses and long spoons on hand, but the sundae will taste just as good in a wine glass. Look for fan-shaped wafer cookies online, or use rolled wafers.

Zabaglione

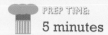
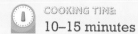
nutritional information per serving	150 cal, 6g fat, 1.5g sat fat, 16g total sugars, trace salt

Zabaglione is a traditional Italian dessert made from whisked eggs and sugar, flavored with a sweet wine called Marsala.

INGREDIENTS

4 egg yolks
⅓ cup sugar
⅓ cup Marsala
amaretti cookies, to serve

1. Put the egg yolks and sugar in a large heatproof bowl. Whisk for 1 minute, then gently whisk in the Marsala. Set the bowl over a saucepan of gently simmering water and whisk vigorously for 10–15 minutes, until thick, creamy, and foamy.

2. Pour into four serving glasses. Serve immediately with amaretti cookies.

Lemon Mousse

 SERVES 4   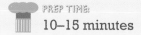 PREP TIME: 10–15 minutes    COOKING TIME: No cooking

nutritional information per serving	442 cal, 40g fat, 25g sat fat, 15g total sugars, 0.1g salt

An old-fashioned English dessert, this is mentioned in the works of Shakespeare, referred to as "posset." With the delicious tang of lemon, these simple ingredients can be turned into the perfect dinner-party finale.

INGREDIENTS

grated rind and juice of
1 large lemon
¼ cup dry white wine
¼ cup sugar
1¼ cups heavy cream
2 egg whites
lemon zest, to decorate
thin butter cookies, to serve

1. Put the lemon rind and juice, wine, and sugar in a bowl. Mix until the sugar has dissolved. Add the cream and beat with a handheld electric mixer until soft peaks form.

2. Beat the egg whites in a separate bowl, until stiff but not dry. Gently fold into the cream mixture.

3. Spoon the mixture into four serving glasses. Decorate with lemon zest and serve immediately with thin butter cookies.

1

1

2

SOMETHING
DIFFERENT
You can use orange
instead of lemon
for this recipe and
serve with shortbread
instead of delicate
butter cookies.

Nectarine Crunch

 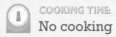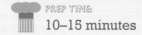

nutritional information per tart	400 cal, 11.5g fat, 2.5g sat fat, 44g total sugars, 0.2g salt

Serve this crunchy, fruity concoction as a summery dessert or as a speedily prepared brunch dish. Peaches would be an excellent substitute for nectarines, too.

INGREDIENTS

4 nectarines
2 tablespoons peach preserves
2 tablespoons peach juice
1½ cups raisin and nut granola
1¼ cups low-fat plain yogurt

1. Cut the nectarines in half, then remove and discard the stones. Chop the flesh into bite-size pieces and reserve a few slices for decoration.

2. Put the preserves and peach juice in a bowl and mix together.

3. Put a few of the nectarine pieces in the bottom of three sundae glasses. Top with half the granola and a spoonful of the yogurt. Add a few more of the nectarine pieces and spoon a little of the preserves mixture over the fruit. Repeat the layers with the remaining ingredients, finishing with a spoonful of yogurt. Sprinkle any remaining granola over the top of each sundae.

4. Decorate with the reserved nectarine pieces and serve immediately.

1

2

3

Quick Tiramisu

 SERVES 4  PREP TIME: 10–15 minutes  COOKING TIME: No cooking

nutritional information per serving	400 cal, 27g fat, 18g sat fat, 21g total sugars, 0.2g salt

The word "tiramisu" is Italian for "pick me up," and there's no doubt this dreamy, creamy dessert, flavored with dark rum, does just that for those who taste it.

INGREDIENTS

8 ounces mascarpone cheese
1 egg, separated
2 tablespoons plain yogurt
2 tablespoons sugar
2 tablespoons dark rum
2 tablespoons cold strong black coffee, cooled to room temperature
8 ladyfingers
2 tablespoons grated semisweet dark chocolate

1. Put the mascarpone cheese, egg yolk, and yogurt in a large bowl and beat together until smooth.

2. Whisk the egg white in a separate bowl until stiff but not dry. Add the sugar and gently fold into the mascarpone mixture. Divide half the mascarpone mixture among four sundae glasses.

3. Pour the rum and coffee into a shallow dish and mix well. Dip the ladyfingers into the rum mixture, break into bite-size pieces, and divide among the glasses.

4. Stir any remaining coffee mixture into the remaining mascarpone mixture and divide among the glasses. Sprinkle with the grated chocolate. Serve immediately, or cover and chill until required.

BE PREPARED
Although this is a
quick version of the
dessert and can be
eaten right away,
it can be prepared
in advance and
chilled until
required to let the
flavors mingle.

Caramel Pecan Apples

 SERVES 4

 PREP TIME:
5 minutes

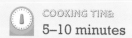 COOKING TIME:
5–10 minutes

nutritional information per serving	442 cal, 21g fat, 10g sat fat, 35g total sugars, 0.3g salt

Toasted brioche is the perfect base to top with buttery apples, flavored with a hint of cinnamon. Pecans add a crunchy topping to this simple yet satisfying dessert that everyone will love.

INGREDIENTS

4 tablespoons unsalted butter

¼ cup firmly packed light brown sugar

4 crisp apples, such as pippin or McIntosh, cored and cut into wedges

1 teaspoon ground cinnamon

4 thick slices of brioche

¼ cup rum or apple juice

⅓ cup pecans

1. Melt the butter in a skillet and stir in the sugar, apples, and cinnamon. Cook over medium heat, stirring occasionally, for 5–6 minutes, until caramelized and golden.

2. Meanwhile, toast the brioche on both sides until golden.

3. Stir the rum and pecans into the skillet and cook for an additional minute.

4. Transfer the toasted brioche to warm serving plates. Spoon the apple mixture over the brioche and serve immediately.

1

1

3

BE PREPARED *Keep a brioche in your freezer already sliced so you can use only as much as you need.*

Mini Apple Gratins

 SERVES 4    PREP TIME: 5 minutes    COOKING TIME: 15 minutes

nutritional information per serving	304 cal, 14g fat, 8g sat fat, 27g total sugars, trace salt

Try something sweet and fruity for dessert, enriched with maple syrup and a hint of allspice.

INGREDIENTS

2 large cooking apples, such as Granny Smith, peeled, cored, and chopped

3 tablespoons maple syrup

juice of ½ lemon

½ teaspoon ground allspice

4 tablespoons unsalted butter

1 cup rolled oats

3 tablespoons light brown sugar

heavy cream, to serve

1. Preheat the oven to 425°F. Put a baking sheet in the oven to preheat. Place the apples, maple syrup, lemon juice, and allspice in a large saucepan over medium heat. Bring to a boil, stirring occasionally, then cover and cook for 5 minutes, until tender.

2. Meanwhile, melt the butter in a small saucepan over medium heat. Remove from the heat and stir in the oats and sugar.

3. Divide the apples among four 1-cup ovenproof dishes and sprinkle with the oat mixture. Bake on the baking sheet in the preheated oven for 10 minutes, until lightly browned and bubbling.

4. Serve immediately with heavy cream.

FREEZING TIP
Bake the crumble topping, let cool, and freeze for up to 3 months in a freezer bag.
Defrost before reheating in the oven or microwave.

Mini Fruit Tarts

 MAKES 8    PREP TIME:
10 minutes    COOKING TIME:
10–12 minutes

nutritional information per tart | 241 cal, 14g fat, 7g sat fat, 7.5g total sugars, 0.6g salt

These irresistible little sweet tarts made are with fresh fruit-perfect for a simple dessert or afternoon treat.

INGREDIENTS

1 (18-ounce) package ready-to-bake puff pastry sheets

2 nectarines, halved, pitted, and thinly sliced

1 tablespoon butter, melted

2 tablespoons demerara sugar or other raw sugar

½ teaspoon ground cinnamon

crème fraîche or whipped cream, to serve

1. Preheat the oven to 425°F. Use a 4-inch round cutter to the stamp out eight circles from the pastry and place on a baking sheet.

2. Arrange the slices of nectarine overlapping on the circles of pastry, leaving ½-inch clear around the edges. Brush the slices with the melted butter. Mix the sugar and cinnamon, then sprinkle over the fruit.

3. Bake in the preheated oven for 10–12 minutes, until well-risen, golden brown, and bubbling.

4. Serve immediately with crème fraîche.

SOMETHING DIFFERENT
Prepare to the end of step 2, moisten the pastry edges, and place another circle of pastry on top. Press to seal, make a steam vent, and bake for 15-20 minutes.

Chocolate Pudding

 SERVES 6    PREP TIME: 10 minutes   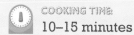 COOKING TIME: 10–15 minutes

nutritional information
per serving   236 cal, 13g fat, 8g sat fat, 19g total sugars, 0.6g salt

This is a rich chocolate pudding that's quick to make and wonderful to eat. Stir in some sliced banana for a complete treat.

INGREDIENTS

½ cup sugar

¼ cup unsweetened cocoa powder

2 tablespoons cornstarch

pinch of salt

1½ cups milk

1 egg, beaten

4 tablespoons butter

½ teaspoon vanilla extract

heavy cream, to serve

1. Mix the sugar, cocoa powder, cornstarch, and salt in a heatproof bowl and set aside.

2. Pour the milk into a saucepan and heat over medium heat until just simmering. Do not bring to a boil.

3. Keeping the pan over medium heat, spoon a little of the simmering milk into the sugar mixture and blend, then stir this mixture into the milk in the pan. Beat in the egg and half the butter, then reduce the heat to low.

4. Simmer for 5–8 minutes, stirring frequently, until the mixture thickens. Remove from the heat and add the vanilla extract and the remaining butter, stirring until the butter melts and is absorbed.

5. Transfer to serving bowls. Drizzle with heavy cream and serve immediately.

1

2

3

Chocolate Orange Pots

 SERVES 4   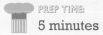 PREP TIME: 5 minutes    COOKING TIME: 5 minutes

nutritional information per serving	387 cal, 27g fat, 18g sat fat, 30g total sugars, trace salt

When you want the perfect ending to a great meal, what could be better than a little dish of indulgence? Chocolate and orange are great partners in this simple yet sophisticated dessert.

INGREDIENTS

1 orange

4 ounces semisweet dark chocolate, broken into pieces

2 tablespoons unsalted butter

3 tablespoons maple syrup

1 tablespoon orange liqueur

½ cup crème fraîche

strips of orange zest, to decorate

1. Cut the white pith and peel from the orange and lift out the segments, catching the juices in a bowl. Cut the segments into small chunks.

2. Heat the chocolate, butter, maple syrup, liqueur, and reserved orange juice in a small saucepan over low heat, stirring occasionally until smooth. Stir in ¼ cup of the crème fraîche and the orange chunks.

3. Transfer to individual serving dishes. Top each with a spoonful of the remaining crème fraîche, decorate with strips of orange zest, and serve immediately.

1

2

3

Pineapple Dessert

 SERVES 6   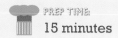 PREP TIME: 15 minutes   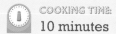 COOKING TIME: 10 minutes

nutritional information per serving	182 cal, 1g fat, 0.5g sat fat, 33g total sugars, trace salt

This is a wonderful dessert of sliced fresh pineapple served warm, topped with fruit and maple syrup.

INGREDIENTS

1 pineapple
¼ cup golden raisins
2 tablespoons raisins
¼ cup maple syrup
¼ cup white rum
1 egg yolk
1 tablespoon cornstarch
½ teaspoon vanilla extract
¼ teaspoon ground ginger
2 egg whites
2 tablespoons light brown sugar

1. Preheat the oven to 475°F. Cut off the leafy top and the bottom of the pineapple and discard. Stand the pineapple upright and slice off the skin. Remove any remaining "eyes" with the tip of a small sharp knife. Cut in half lengthwise and remove the hard, woody core, then finely slice the flesh.

2. Arrange the pineapple slices in a large ovenproof dish and sprinkle the golden raisins and raisins over it. Drizzle with half the maple syrup and half the rum. Bake in the preheated oven for 5 minutes.

3. Meanwhile, place the remaining maple syrup and rum, egg yolk, cornstarch, vanilla extract, and ginger in a large bowl and mix together.

4. Whisk the egg whites in a separate bowl, until stiff but not dry. Gently fold the egg yolk mixture into the egg whites.

5. Spread the topping over the hot pineapple, sprinkle the sugar over the pineapple, and bake in the preheated oven for 5 minutes, until golden brown.

6. Transfer to warm serving plates and serve immediately.

2

4

5

Broiled Cinnamon Oranges

 SERVES 4    PREP TIME: 5 minutes    COOKING TIME: 3–5 minutes

nutritional information per serving	88 cal, 0.2g fat, 0g sat fat, 20g total sugars, trace salt

Halved oranges, topped with cinnamon and sugar, will smell absolutely delicious as they grill and are a simple, healthy way to end a meal. They are equally suitable for a breakfast menu, too.

INGREDIENTS

4 large oranges
1 teaspoon ground cinnamon
1 tablespoon demerara sugar or other raw sugar

1. Preheat the broiler to high. Cut the oranges in half and discard any seeds. Using a sharp knife, carefully cut the flesh away from the skin by cutting around the edge of the fruit. Cut across the segments to loosen the flesh into bite-size pieces that will then spoon out easily.

2. Arrange the orange halves, cut-side up, in a shallow, flameproof dish. Mix the cinnamon with the sugar in a small bowl and sprinkle evenly over the orange halves.

3. Cook under the preheated broiler for 3–5 minutes, until the sugar has caramelized and is golden and bubbling. Serve immediately.

1

2

2

GOES WELL WITH

Top with plain or
honey-flavored yogurt
for a special treat.

Grilled Bananas

 SERVES 4

 PREP TIME:
10 minutes

 COOKING TIME:
10 minutes

nutritional information per serving	521 cal, 40g fat, 28g sat fat, 32g total sugars, trace salt

For the taste of the Caribbean, try these bananas grilled to perfection with coconut and lime.

INGREDIENTS

2-ounce block of creamed coconut (available from Caribbean or Asian stores), chopped, or 1 teaspoon coconut extract

⅔ cup heavy cream

4 bananas

juice and finely grated rind of 1 lime, plus 1 lime, cut into wedges

1 tablespoon vegetable oil or peanut oil

¾ cup dried coconut

1. Preheat the broiler to medium. Put the creamed coconut and cream in a small saucepan over low heat, stirring continuously, until the coconut has dissolved. Remove from the heat and let cool for 10 minutes, then beat until thick. Alternatively, add the coconut extract to the heavy cream and beat until thick.

2. Preheat a ridged grill pan over high heat. Peel the bananas and toss in the lime juice and rind. Brush the preheated grill pan with the oil, add the bananas, and cook, turning once, for 2–3 minutes, until softened and browned. Add the lime wedges halfway through the cooking time.

3. Toast the dried coconut on a piece of aluminum foil under the preheated broiler until lightly browned. Serve the bananas with the lime wedges and coconut cream, sprinkled with the dried coconut.

1

1
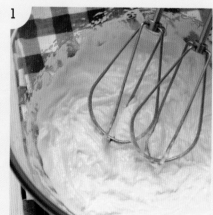

2

Almond & Strawberry Pancakes

 SERVES 4　　 PREP TIME: 15 minutes　　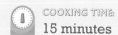 COOKING TIME: 15 minutes

nutritional information per serving	671 cal, 49g fat, 25g sat fat, 17g total sugars, 1g salt

Light, fluffy pancakes made in minutes and topped with strawberries and crème fraîche are a dream come true for the dessert-lover.

INGREDIENTS

1¼ cups all-purpose flour
1½ teaspoon baking powder
pinch of salt
2 tablespoons sugar
1 cup milk
1 extra-large egg
2 tablespoons melted butter
2 tablespoons light cream
2 tablespoons ground almonds
1 teaspoon almond extract
sunflower oil, for greasing

filling & topping

1 cup crème fraîche or whipped cream
1½ cups sliced, hulled strawberries
confectioners' sugar, for dusting
3 tablespoons slivered almonds, toasted, to serve

1. Sift the flour, baking powder, salt, and sugar into a bowl. Add the milk, egg, butter, cream, almonds, and almond extract and beat to a smooth batter. Let stand for 5 minutes.

2. Lightly grease a skillet with the oil and place over medium heat. Spoon the batter into the skillet, creating small, round pancakes. Cook until bubbles appear on the uppermost surface of the pancakes.

3. Turn the pancakes over with a spatula and cook the other side, until golden brown. Repeat this process until all of the remaining batter has been used. Meanwhile, keep the cooked pancakes warm.

4. Stack the pancakes, three at a time, alternating them with crème fraîche and strawberries. Top with a spoonful of crème fraîche and more sliced strawberries. Sprinkle with confectioners' sugar and slivered almonds and serve immediately.

1

4

4

Raspberry & Croissant Bread Puddings

 SERVES 4    PREP TIME: 10 minutes    COOKING TIME: 25 minutes

nutritional information per serving	441 cal, 26g fat, 13g sat fat, 18g total sugars, 0.9g salt

Store-bought croissants make a quick bread and butter pudding dessert that everyone will love.

INGREDIENTS

2 tablespoons unsalted butter, melted

4 croissants

2 cups fresh raspberries

¼ cup maple syrup

1½ cups milk

2 extra-large eggs, beaten

1 teaspoon vanilla extract

freshly grated nutmeg, for sprinkling

1. Preheat the oven to 425°F. Place a baking sheet in the oven to preheat. Brush four 1½-cup ramekins (individual ceramic dishes) with half the butter.

2. Chop the croissants into bite-size chunks. Mix with the raspberries and divide among the dishes. Spoon over the maple syrup.

3. Pour the milk into a small saucepan place it over low heat and bring almost to a boil. Pour into a heatproof bowl, then quickly beat in the eggs and vanilla extract.

4. Pour the milk mixture evenly over the dishes, pressing the croissants down lightly.

5. Drizzle with the remaining butter and sprinkle a little nutmeg over each dish. Bake in the preheated oven for about 20 minutes, until lightly set. Serve immediately.

2

3

5

Caramel Popcorn

  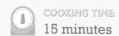

nutritional information per serving	487 cal, 30g fat, 14g sat fat, 41g total sugars, 0.4g salt

This is a truly sweet way to eat popcorn! Coated with syrup, brown sugar, and nuts, then drizzled with melted chocolate, this is a treat that won't be forgotten.

INGREDIENTS

1 tablespoon sunflower oil, plus extra for greasing

½ cup popcorn

6 tablespoons butter

½ cup firmly packed light brown sugar

2 tablespoons light corn syrup

3 tablespoons chopped pecans,

2 ounces milk chocolate, melted

1. Preheat the oven to 325°F. Lightly grease a large baking sheet with oil. Heat the remaining oil in a large saucepan over high heat. Add the popcorn, cover, and cook for 3–4 minutes, shaking occasionally, until all the popcorn has popped.

2. Heat the butter, sugar, and light corn syrup in a small saucepan over medium heat until the butter has melted. Bring to a boil and let the mixture bubble rapidly for 1 minute. Quickly pour the hot caramel over the warm popcorn, add the chopped pecan nuts, and mix thoroughly.

3. Spread the popcorn over the baking sheet and bake in the preheated oven for 10 minutes. Let cool, then break into smaller pieces. Drizzle the melted chocolate over the caramel popcorn and let stand until set. Serve in small bowls, paper cones, or cupcake liners.

COOK'S NOTE
Children love to make popcorn, but with this recipe they will need supervision because the syrup mixture will be hot.

Churros

 SERVES 6    PREP TIME: 15 minutes   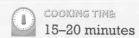 COOKING TIME: 15–20 minutes

nutritional information per serving	553 cal, 41g fat, 16g sat fat, 23g total sugars, 0.4g salt

Some say these doughnuts originated in Spain, others say South America, and they can be bought freshly made in French markets, too! Whoever invented them, they are a treat to eat, dipped in a silky chocolate sauce.

INGREDIENTS

1 stick butter
1¼ cups all-purpose flour, sifted
2 extra-large eggs, beaten
sunflower oil, for deep frying
¼ cup sugar
1 teaspoon ground cinnamon

chocolate sauce

4 ounces semisweet dark chocolate, broken into pieces
1 tablespoon light corn syrup
1 tablespoon butter
¼ cup milk

1. Heat the butter and 1¼ cups of water in a large saucepan over medium heat until the butter has melted. Bring to a boil, remove from the heat, and add the flour. Beat thoroughly until the mixture is smooth. Cool for 10 minutes, then gradually beat in the eggs to make a thick paste.

2. Fill a deep skillet halfway with sunflower oil. Heat the oil until it reaches 350°F, or until a cube of bread browns in 30 seconds. Spoon the paste into a pastry bag fitted with a star tip and pipe 4–5 lengths of the paste into the hot oil. Cook for 2–3 minutes, or until crisp and golden. Remove and drain on paper towels. Keep warm while cooking the remaining churros.

3. Put the sugar and cinnamon in a large, shallow dish and mix well. Toss the warm churros in the sugar to coat lightly.

4. To make the chocolate sauce, put all the ingredients in a heatproof bowl set over a saucepan of simmering water, stirring occasionally until melted and smooth.

5. Transfer the churros to serving bowls and serve immediately with the chocolate sauce.

1

2

4

Syrup Cake with Vanilla Pudding

 SERVES 4    PREP TIME: 10 minutes    COOKING TIME: 10 minutes

nutritional information per serving	519 cal, 30g fat, 18g sat fat, 33g total sugars, 1.3g salt

Quickly made in the microwave, this syrup-topped cake served with vanilla pudding will warm you on a cold day.

INGREDIENTS

1 stick butter, plus extra for greasing

¼ cup light corn syrup

½ cup sugar

2 eggs, lightly beaten

1 cup all-purpose flour

2½ teaspoons baking powder

about 2 tablespoons warm water

prepared vanilla pudding, warmed, to serve

1. Grease a deep 1½-quart ovenproof bowl with butter. Spoon the light corn syrup into the prepared bowl.

2. Beat the remaining butter with the sugar in a bowl until pale and fluffy. Gradually add the eggs, beating well after each addition.

3. Sift together the flour and baking powder, then gently fold into the butter mixture. Add enough water to produce a soft, dropping consistency. Spoon the mixture into the bowl and level the surface.

4. Cover with microwave-safe plastic wrap, leaving a small space to let the air escape. Cook in a microwave oven on high, for 4 minutes, then remove and let the cake stand for 5 minutes while it continues to cook.

5. Invert the cake onto a serving plate. Serve immediately with warm vanilla pudding.

1

2

4

SOMETHING DIFFERENT
Replace the syrup in the recipe with your favorite preserves, or even stewed fruit.

Blueberry & Vanilla Muffins

 MAKES 18

 PREP TIME: 10 minutes

 COOKING TIME: 15 minutes

nutritional information per muffin	60 cal, 2g fat, 0.3g sat fat, 5g total sugars, 0.2g salt

The juicy berries in this recipe burst during cooking to color and flavor the muffins.

INGREDIENTS

1 cup all-purpose flour
2 teaspoons baking powder
⅓ cup sugar
½ cup blueberries
2 teaspoons vanilla extract
1 egg
½ cup buttermilk
2 tablespoons vegetable oil
vanilla sugar, for dusting

1. Preheat the oven to 375°F. Cut out eighteen 3½-inch squares from parchment paper. Line two mini muffin pans, creasing the squares to fit so that they form eighteen paper liners. Don't worry if they lift out of the cups slightly; the weight of the muffin batter will hold them in place.

2. Sift the flour and baking powder into a mixing bowl. Stir in the sugar and blueberries. In a separate mixing bowl, beat together the vanilla, egg, buttermilk, and oil with a fork until evenly combined.

3. Gently fold the buttermilk mixture into the flour, until loosely combined.

4. Spoon the batter into the paper liners and sprinkle with a little of the vanilla sugar. Bake in the preheated oven for 15 minutes, or until risen and just firm to the touch. Let the muffins cool in the pans for 2 minutes, then transfer them to a wire rack to cool. Serve warm or cold, dusted with extra vanilla sugar.

1

2

4

Double Chocolate Muffins

nutritional information per muffin	119 cal, 7g fat, 4g sat fat, 8g total sugars, 0.2g salt

Because these muffins are tiny, it's only right that they're as packed with as much chocolate as possible!

INGREDIENTS

3 tablespoons cocoa powder

½ cup all-purpose flour

¾ teaspoon baking powder

2 tablespoons light brown sugar

3 ounces milk chocolate, coarsely chopped

1 egg

3 tablespoons milk

3 tablespoons lightly salted butter, melted

2 ounces semisweet dark chocolate, coarsely chopped

1. Preheat the oven to 375°F. Line a mini muffin pan with 12 paper liners.

2. Sift the cocoa powder, flour, and baking powder into a mixing bowl. Stir in the light brown sugar and milk chocolate. In a separate mixing bowl, beat together the egg, milk, and butter with a fork until they are evenly combined.

3. Gentle fold the egg mixture into the flour, until loosely combined.

4. Spoon the mixture into the paper liners. Bake in the preheated oven for 15 minutes, or until risen and just firm to the touch. Let the muffins cool in the pan for 2 minutes, then transfer them to a wire rack to cool.

5. Put the dark chocolate in a heatproof bowl, set over a saucepan of gently simmering water, and heat until melted. Drizzle the melted chocolate over the muffins and serve warm or cold.

2

4

5

COOK'S NOTE
Any muffins that
are not eaten fresh
from the oven can
be kept for two
days in an
airtight container.

Molten-Centered Lava Chocolate Cupcakes

 MAKES 8

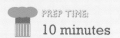 PREP TIME:
10 minutes

 COOKING TIME:
20 minutes

nutritional information
per cupcake   167 cal, 9g fat, 3g sat fat, 11g total sugars, 0.3g salt

Melting chocolate in the center of a light and crumbly cupcake is bound to be everyone's idea of a perfect anytime treat.

INGREDIENTS

¼ cup soft margarine

¼ cup sugar

1 extra-large egg

⅔ cup all-purpose flour,

1 teaspoon baking powder

1 tablespoon unsweetened cocoa powder,

2 ounces semisweet dark chocolate

confectioners' sugar, sifted, for dusting

1. Preheat the oven to 375°F. Line a muffin pan with eight muffin cases.

2. Put the margarine, sugar, and egg in a large bowl. Sift the flour and baking powder on top, and use an electric handheld mixer to beat the mixture until just smooth.

3. Spoon half of the batter into the muffin cups. Using a teaspoon, make an indentation in the center of each cake. Break the chocolate evenly into 8 squares and place a piece in each indentation, then spoon the remaining muffin batter on top.

4. Bake the cupcakes in the preheated oven for 20 minutes, or until well risen and just firm to the touch. Let cool in the pan for 2 minutes, then serve warm, dusted with confectioners' sugar.

Giant Chocolate Chunk Cookies

 MAKES 12   PREP TIME: 10 minutes    COOKING TIME: 15–20 minutes

nutritional information per cookie	266 cal, 10g fat, 6g sat fat, 22g total sugars, 0.5g salt

There are so many occasions when a home-baked cookie is just what's needed, and this recipe is the one to use.

INGREDIENTS

1 stick butter, softened

½ cup granulated sugar

½ cup firmly packed light brown sugar

2 extra-large eggs, lightly beaten

1 teaspoon vanilla extract

2¼ cups all-purpose flour

1 teaspoon baking soda

10 ounces milk chocolate, broken into pieces

1. Preheat the oven to 350°F. Line four large baking sheets with parchment paper.

2. Put the butter and sugars in a large bowl and beat together until pale and creamy. Beat the eggs and vanilla extract into the mixture until smooth. Sift in the flour and baking soda and beat until well mixed. Stir in the chocolate chunks.

3. Drop 12 large spoonfuls of the dough onto the prepared baking sheets, allowing for plenty of space to spread.

4. Bake in the preheated oven for 15–20 minutes, or until set and golden brown. Let cool on the baking sheets for 2 minutes, then transfer the cookies to a wire rack to cool completely.

2

2

3

COOK'S NOTE
Store baked cookies
in an airtight
container at room
temperature for up
to a week—if they
last that long!

Brandy Snaps

 MAKES 20   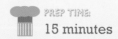 PREP TIME: 15 minutes    COOKING TIME: 30–35 minutes

nutritional information per snap	110 cal, 8g fat, 5g sat fat, 6g total sugars, trace salt

This is a wonderful dessert, filled with whipped cream. They are good enough to serve to special guests.

INGREDIENTS

6 tablespoons unsalted butter
½ cup superfine sugar
3 tablespoons light corn syrup
⅔ cup all-purpose flour
1 teaspoon ground ginger
1 tablespoon brandy
finely grated rind of ½ lemon

filling

⅔ cup heavy cream
1 tablespoon brandy (optional)
1 tablespoon confectioners' sugar

1. Preheat the oven to 325°F. Line three large baking sheets with parchment paper.

2. Place the butter, sugar, and corn syrup in a saucepan and heat gently over low heat, stirring occasionally, until smooth. Remove from the heat and let cool slightly.

3. Sift the flour and ginger into the pan and beat until smooth, then stir in the brandy and lemon rind. Drop 20 small spoonfuls of the mixture onto the prepared baking sheets, allowing plenty of space for spreading.

4. Bake one baking sheet at a time in the preheated oven for 10–12 minutes, or until the snaps are golden brown. Remove the first baking sheet from the oven. Let cool for about 30 seconds, then lift each snap with a spatula and wrap around the handle of a wooden spoon. If the snaps become too firm to wrap, return to the oven for about 30 seconds to soften.

5. When firm, remove the snaps from the spoon handles and finish cooling on a wire rack. Repeat with the remaining snaps, one baking sheet at a time.

6. To make the filling, whip the cream with the brandy, if using, and confectioners' sugar until thick. Chill in the refrigerator until required.

7. Just before serving, pipe the cream mixture into both ends of each brandy snap.

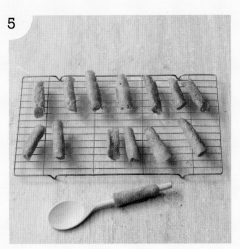

Index